BATSFORD CHESS COURSE

MICHAEL BASMAN

COLLIER BOOKS

MACMILLAN PUBLISHING COMPANY

NEW YORK

Collier Books
Macmillan Publishing Company
866 Third Avenue, New York, NY 10022
Collier Macmillan Canada, Inc.

Library of Congress Cataloging-in-Publication Data

Basman, Michael.
    Batsford chess course/Michael Basman. -- 1st Collier Books ed.
        p.   cm.
    ISBN 0-02-030377-7
    1. Chess.   I. Title
GV1449.5.B37   1990   89-31922   CIP
794.1'2 – – dc20

Macmillan books are available at special discounts for bulk purchases for sales promotions,
premiums, fund-raising, or educational use. For details contact:

Special Sales Director
Macmillan Publishing Company
866 Third Avenue
New York, NY 10022

First Collier Books Edition 1990

10 9 8 7 6 5 4 3 2 1

Printed in Great Britain

CONTENTS

HOW TO PLAY CHESS

CHESS is a game played by two players on a board of 64 squares, each side moving alternately.

Each side has an army of sixteen men: two rooks, two knights, two bishops, eight pawns, one queen and one king. They are set up at the start of the game as in diagram A.

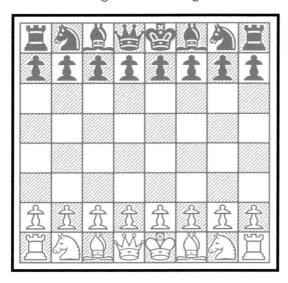

Diagram A

The moves of the pieces

The rook moves on the horizontals and verticals, as many squares as it wishes, but it cannot pass men in its path.

The bishop moves on the diagonals, also as many squares as it wishes. It cannot pass men in its path.

The moves of these two pieces are shown in diagram B.

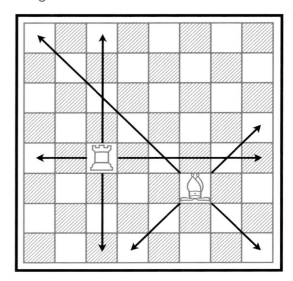

Diagram B

The queen combines the moves of rook and bishop, moving vertically, horizontally or diagonally, as many squares as it wants to. The queen's move is shown in diagram C.

The king can only move one square at a time in any direction. Its move is also shown in diagram C.

The pawn is the only man that cannot move backwards; it stands on the second row and advances one square at a time, except that on the first move it has the option of moving two squares. If the pawn reaches the far row it can be promoted to a queen, knight , rook or bishop.

The knight is the only piece that can jump over men in its path. It also has a peculiar hopping movement, reaching its target square by crossing one square forwards followed by one square diagonally.

The moves of these two men are shown in Diagram D

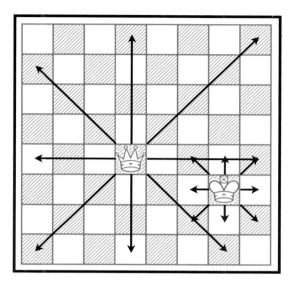

Diagram C

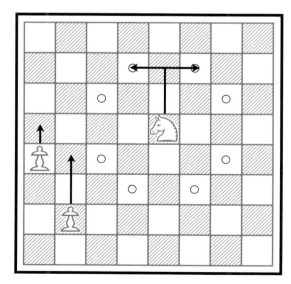

Diagram D

Capturing

Pieces can capture enemy pieces by displacing an enemy piece in their path. They move into the square of the enemy piece and remove it from the board.

In diagram E, the rook can capture the black bishop.

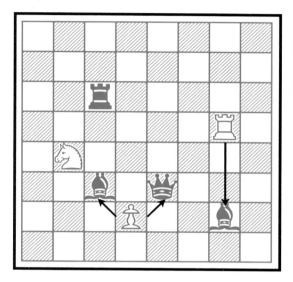

Diagram E

Exception: the knight does not control the squares it passes over, so it can only capture pieces on the squares it might land on.

Exception: pawns cannot capture pieces directly in front of them, only pieces *diagonally* in front of them.

In diagram E, the pawn can capture either the bishop or queen.

Checkmate

A king under attack is said to be in *check*; if he is under attack and cannot escape, this is called *checkmate*, or mate. The side giving checkmate immediately wins the game. You do not actually have to capture the enemy king to win the game; if there is no escape from check, that is enough.

In diagram F, the black king is under attack from the white queen, and the king has no move that does not escape the attack. Any square the king might go to is under attack from the white men. This is checkmate.

Here is another example of checkmate (diagram G).

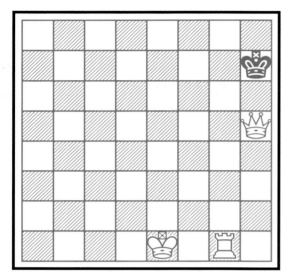

Diagram F

Diagram G

–1–
WRITING MOVES

THE system of recording moves we use is called the *Algebraic Notation*.

The squares

The rows of squares going up the board are called *files*; these are marked 'a' to 'h'.

The rows of squares going sideways are called *ranks*; these are numbered 1 to 8.

By joining up the letters and the numbers you can name every square on the board.

So if you draw a line from the letter 'd' and another from the number '4' (see diagram 1), where the lines meet you have the square 'd4'.

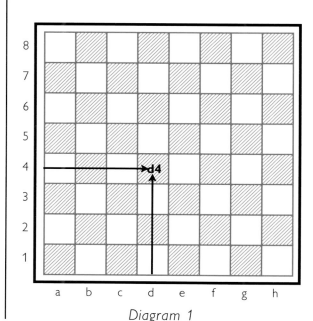

Diagram 1

Practice exercise

Clear your chess board and place:

  a white queen on e4
  a white rook on h5
  a white pawn on b3
  a black queen on b7
  a black knight on f8
  a black pawn on e2

Then check your board with diagram 2 overleaf.

The pieces

Each piece has its own letter.

  K = king
  Q = queen
  R = rook
  N = knight
  B = bishop
No letter is used for a pawn.

Writing moves

If we were moving our rook on c3 to c6 (see diagram 3) we would write the move Rc6
  (R stands for rook, and c6 is the square it is going to)
  Captures are written in the same way, but we put an '×' in the middle: B×h5

In the diagram, the bishop at e2 is capturing the knight at h5. We don't name the piece we have captured, only the square that we captured on.

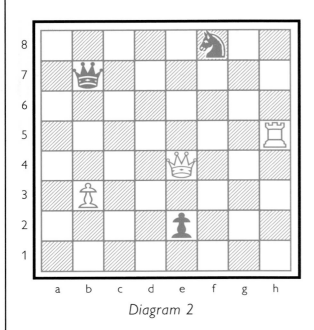

Diagram 2

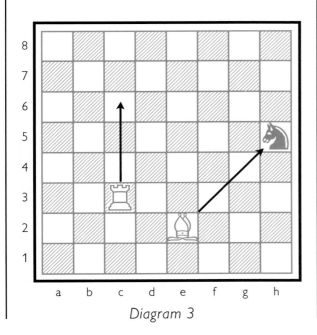

Diagram 3

Pawn moves and captures

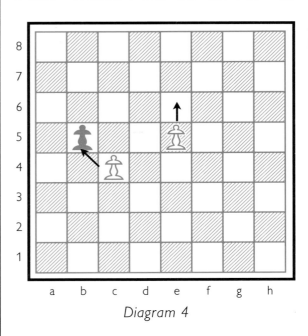

Diagram 4

Pawns have no symbol, so a pawn move would be written by naming the square it went to: e6 (the pawn moved to e6)

Pawn captures are shown by naming the file the pawn came from: c×b5 (see diagram 4). The pawn at c4 captures at b5.

Ambiguous moves

In diagram 5, both rooks can go to e1; if we just write Re1, we do not know which one it was. So we name the *file* the rook is on e.g.

Rfe1   (the rook on f1 moved)
Rae1   (the rook at a1 moved)

When the pieces are on the same file, we name the *rank*. Thus:

N2f3   (the knight on d2 moved)
N4f3   (the knight on d4 moved)

Note: unless at least one pawn has been promoted, ambiguous moves can only occur with rooks and knights!

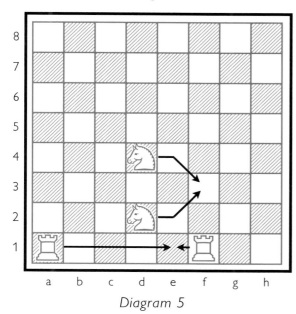

Diagram 5

Other symbols

0 – 0	castles kingside
0 – 0 – 0	castles queenside
+	stands for check (e.g. Bb4+)
++	stands for checkmate (e.g. Q×f7++)
e.p.	captures en passant (see special rules)
!	good move
?	bad move

Writing exercises

Write down the moves as shown by the arrows in the diagrams. Example:

Bh3 R×h5
c4 Qd4+
Ka2 Nd×e4

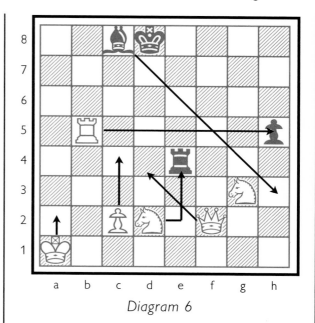

Diagram 6

Practice diagrams

Write the moves down as shown by the arrows in the diagrams. The answers are on page 5.

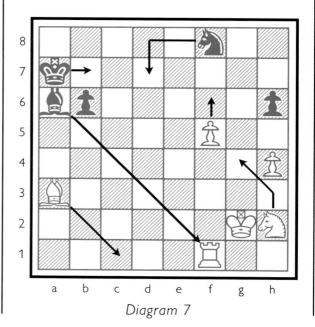

Diagram 7

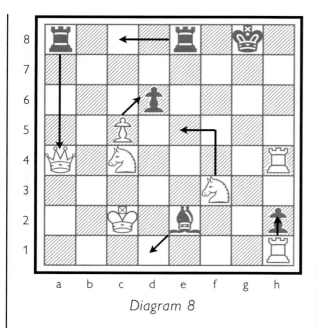

Diagram 8

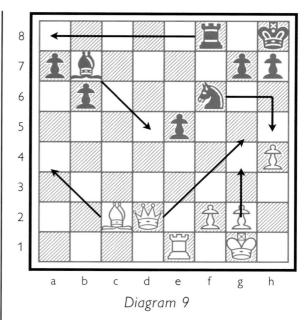

Diagram 9

Test

You have to write down all the moves as shown by the arrows in diagrams 9 – 12. Time yourself. Score 1 point for each move correctly written. Time bonus: for every minute less than 20 that you take to complete the test, give yourself 1 point extra; so if you take 17 minutes, that gives you 3 extra points. The maximum bonus is 6 points. Maximum total score: 30 points. Answers are at the end of the book.

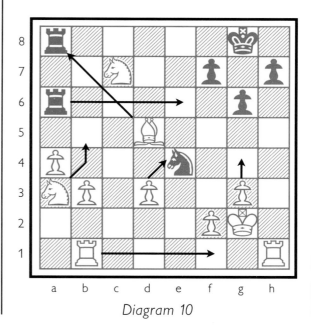

Diagram 10

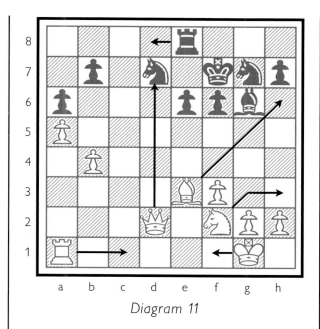

Diagram 11

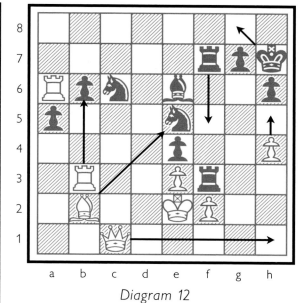

Diagram 12

Answers to practice diagrams 7 and 8.

Diagram 7:

Nd7	Bc1
Kb7	f6
B×f1	Ng4

Diagram 8:

R×a4	Nfe5
Rec8	Bd1+
c×d6	R×h2

-2-
SEEING CAPTURES

SEEING captures is the most important thing in chess – besides checkmating!

Exercise

Write down all the captures you can see for White on this move. One piece may be able to capture more than one enemy piece. Example:

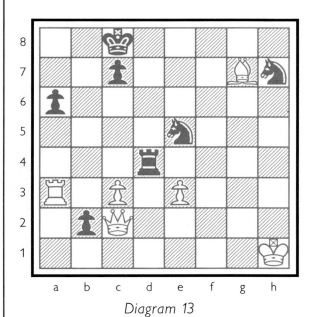

Diagram 13

In this diagram there are six captures.

R×a6	e×d4
B×e5	c×d4
Q×b2	Q×h7

Thinking tip: look at each piece, and look at all the directions it can move in. Thus, for a rook you may have to look in four directions; for a queen, eight directions.

Test

Write down all the captures you can see for White on this move in the next two diagrams. Score 2 points for each capture found.

Time yourself; add 1 bonus point for each minute you take less than 15. The maximum bonus is 6 points. Maximum total score: 30 points.

Answers are at the end of the book.

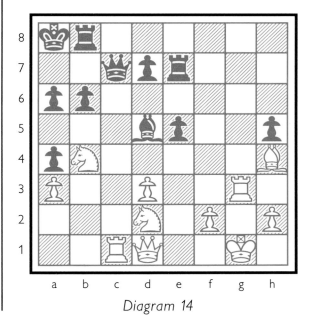

Diagram 14

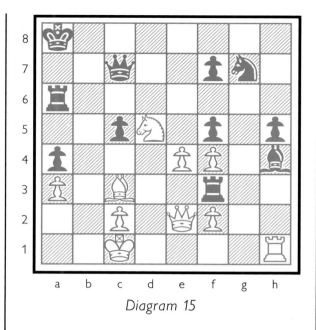

Diagram 15

Value of the pieces

Some pieces are worth more than others, because they are so much stronger and control more squares. For example, the queen, which can attack up to 27 squares, is worth much more than a knight, which can only attack 8 squares at the most.

This table shows the exchange value of each piece:

queen	9 points
rook	5 points
bishop	3 points
knight	3 points
pawn	1 point
king	no exchange value. If you lose him, you lose the game.

N.B. These are *capture* points. They are not the same as the points you score when you do the Bronze course!

In the next tests, besides writing down captures for White, you must arrange them in order of value.

Example:

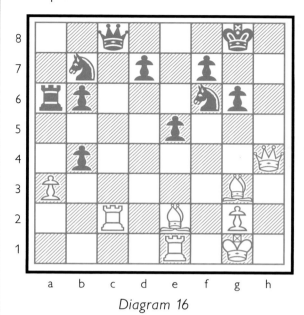

Diagram 16

In diagram 16 there are six captures: Q×b4, Q×f6, B×e5, a×b4, B×a6, R×c8. Arranged in order of value they are:

(1)	R×c8+	wins 9 points
(2)	B×a6	wins 5 points
(3)	Q×f6	wins 3 points
(4)	B×e5	wins 1 point
	Q×b4	wins 1 point
	a×b4	wins 1 point

Test

In the next two diagrams, you should write down all the captures you can see for White *on this move*. In brackets, show the *value* of the piece captured, e.g. Q×d8(3).

Score 2 points for each capture found.

Time yourself: add 1 point for each minute you took less than 15 for both diagrams. The maximum time bonus is 6 points. Maximum score = 36 points.

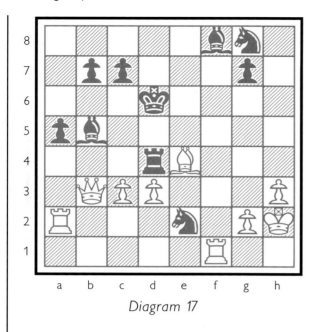

Diagram 17

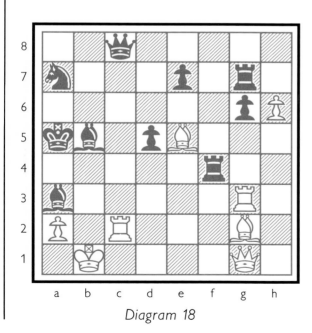

Diagram 18

Capturing and recapturing

What if I take and my opponent takes back? In these exercises, there are lots of enemy pieces to take, but all of them are defended. Example:

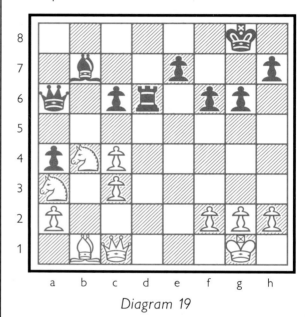

Diagram 19

N×a6 B×a6 (+6)
White captured a queen, worth 9 points, in exchange for a knight, worth 3 points. The total gain, shown in brackets, is 6 points.
R×d6 e×d6 (0)
A swap. White captured a rook, worth 5 points, but also lost a rook, worth the same amount. The total gain, shown in brackets, is zero.
B×g6 h×g6 (−2)
A bad capture, White lost a bishop, worth 3 points, for a pawn, worth 1 point. Total loss: 2 points.

TEST

In diagrams 20 – 23, write down the captures and recaptures that *gain* or *exchange* material for White. Put in brackets the number of material points you have gained as a result. If you have simply swapped equal value pieces, put a zero in brackets.

Score 2 points for each gain and 1 point for each exchange, but *deduct* 2 points if you wrote down a move that loses material. Add 1 bonus point for each minute less than 30 for the test, and deduct 1 point for each minute you took more than 30. The maximum time bonus or deduction is 12 points. Maximum score = 40.

Diagram 20

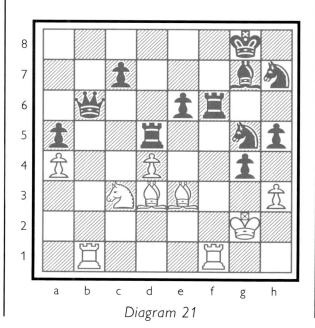

Diagram 21

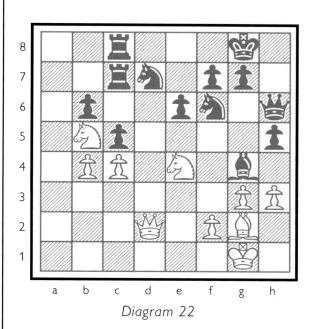

Diagram 22

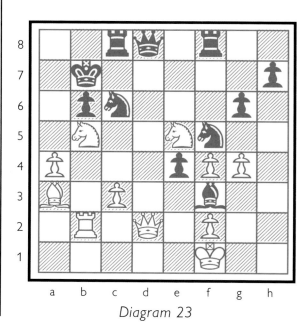

Diagram 23

–3–
CHECKMATING

CHECKMATE is the knockout blow in chess, and just as in boxing, it doesn't matter how many points ahead you are; if your opponent lands the big one, you're dead.

Is this checkmate?

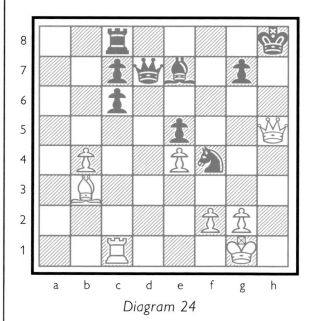

Diagram 24

Can Black *move* the king to a safe square?
No, both g8 and h7 are attacked.
Can Black *block* the attack?
No.
Can Black *capture* the queen?
Yes, by N✕h5.
  So its's not checkmate.

Is this checkmate?

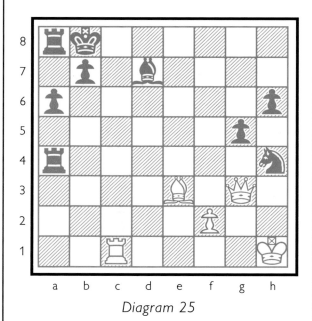

Diagram 25

  Remember the three ways out of check: MOVE, CAPTURE, BLOCK.

MOVE? *No safe square for the king.*
CAPTURE? *Not possible.*
BLOCK? *Yes: Rf4.*
  That wasn't checkmate either.

Is this checkmate?

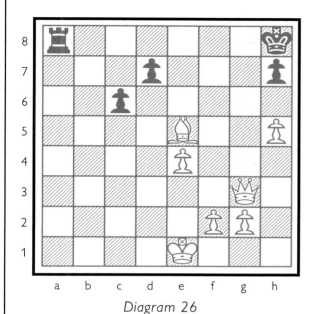

Diagram 26

MOVE? *No.*
CAPTURE? *No.*
BLOCK? *No.*
   It's checkmate.

Exercises in getting out of check

In diagram 27, Kh2 is the only move to get out of check.
   In the following 12 diagrams, you are White, and there is only one move that gets you out of check.
   Score 5 points for each correct solution. Add 1 bonus point for each minute less than 25. Deduct 1 point for each minute you spent over 25. The maximum bonus or deduction is 15 points. Maximum total score = 75. The solutions are at the end of the book.

Example:

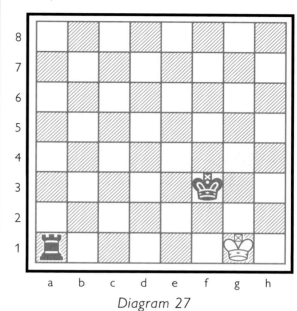

Diagram 27

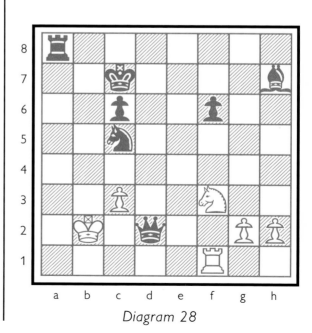

Diagram 28

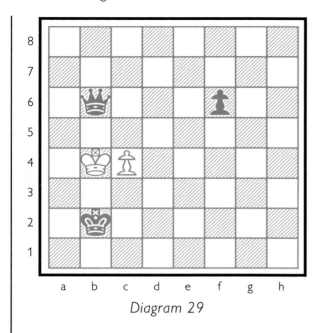

Diagram 29

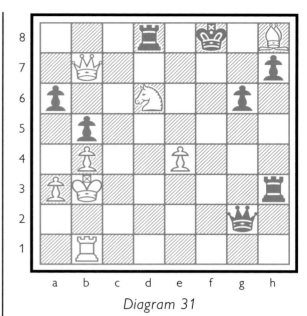

Diagram 31

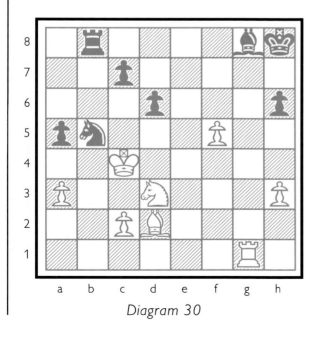

Diagram 30

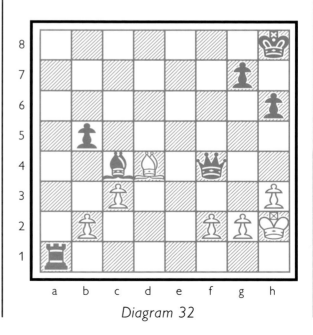

Diagram 32

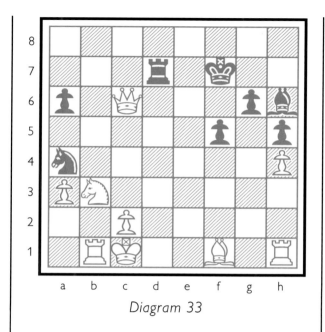

Diagram 33

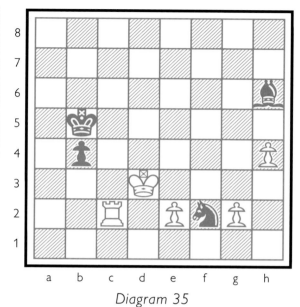

Diagram 35

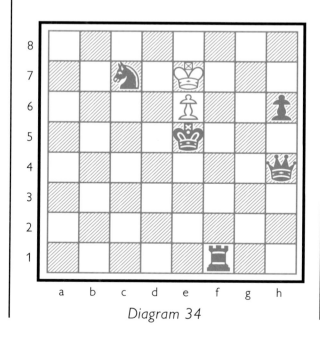

Diagram 34

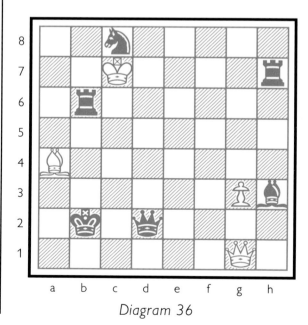

Diagram 36

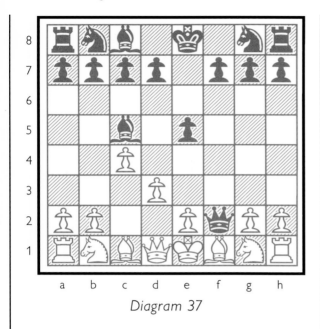

Diagram 37

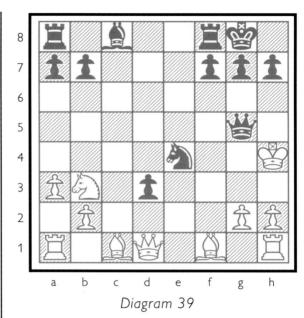

Diagram 39

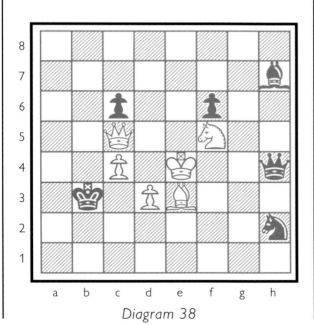

Diagram 38

Checkmating

In the exercises that follow you must find a checkmate in one move. Once you have found a check, you should stop to see if your opponent can escape by MOVING, CAPTURING or BLOCKING.

Example: In diagram 40, White is to play and checkmate in one move.

Solution: Re8++

For a demonstration, I shall show how black meets all of the other checks.

Bf6	Re7	(Block)
Rd3+	Ke7	(Move)
Qg5+	f6	(Block)
Qd5+	Bd7	(Block)

In many cases, there was more than one way to meet the check, but I have shown just one.

Now for the test. All you need to do is find the one move that checkmates Black in diagrams 41 – 46. Score 5 points for each correct solution. Add 1 extra point for each minute below 25 for solving this set. Deduct 1 point for each minute over 25. The maximum bonus or deduction is 20 points. Maximum score = 50. The solutions are at the end of the book.

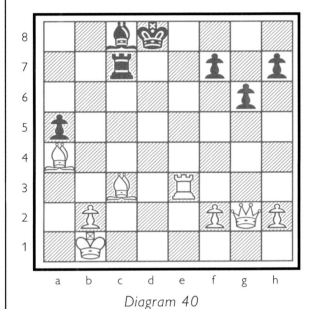

Diagram 40

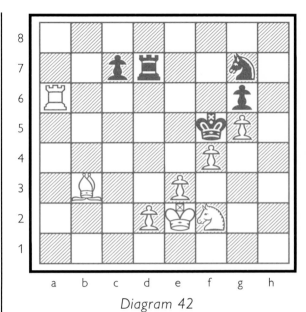

Diagram 42

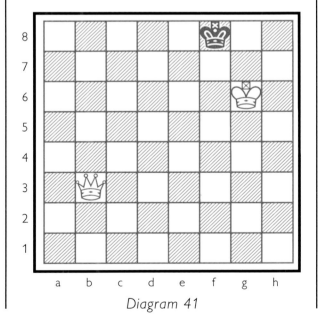

Diagram 41

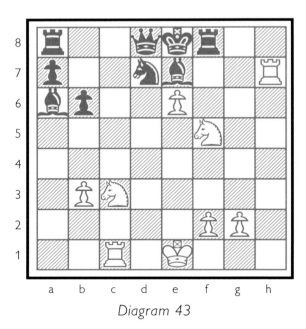

Diagram 43

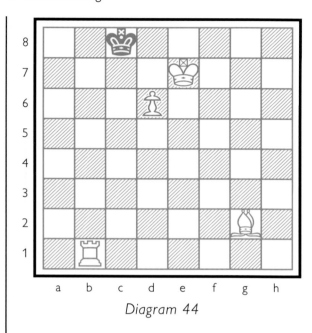

Diagram 44

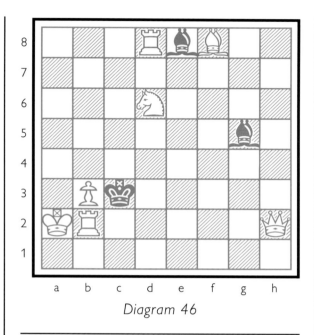

Diagram 46

Is it checkmate?

In diagrams 48 – 53, you are offered four different moves which *might* be checkmate. Show which one *is* checkmate, and also show one defence for Black which avoids checkmate after each of the other 3 tries.

Example:

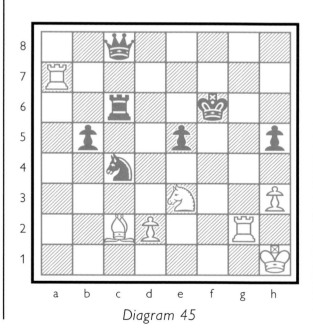

Diagram 45

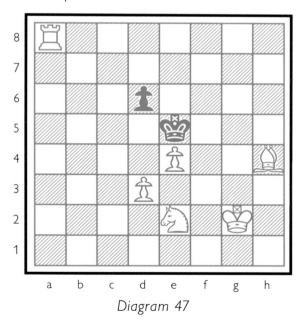

Diagram 47

Suggested moves:
Ra5+
d4+
Re8+
Bg3+

Solution: Re8++
Ra5+   Ke6   (Move)
d4+   K×e4   (Capture)
Bg3+   Ke6   (Move)

Test scoring: 5 points for each diagram for finding the checkmate. 2 points for each move that defends against the check. (Only show one defence per threat). Add 1 bonus point for each minute taken under 25. Deduct 1 point for each minute spent over 25. The maximum bonus or deduction is 14 points. Maximum possible score = 80. The answers are at the end of the book.

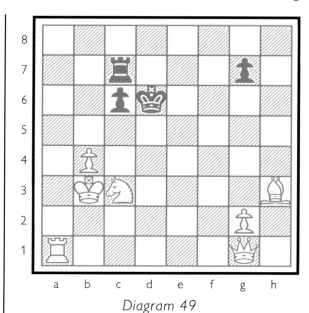

Diagram 49

Qd4+
Rd1+
Ne4+
Qc5+

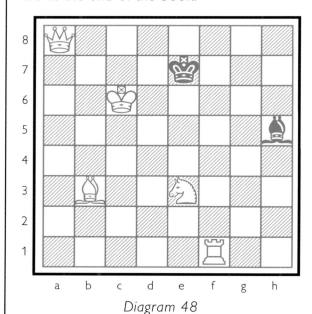

Diagram 48

Qb7+
Nd5+
Qf8+
Rf7+

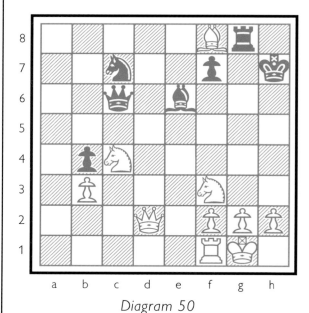

Diagram 50

Qc2+
Qh6+
Ng5+
Qd3+

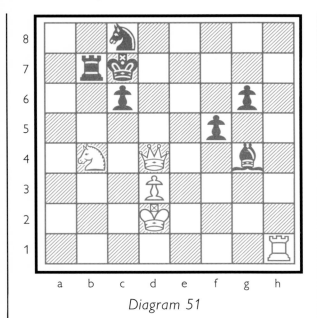

Diagram 51

Na6+
Qe5+
Rh7+
Qg7+

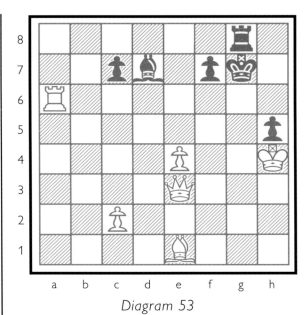

Diagram 53

Bc3+
Qd4+
Qh6+
Rg6+

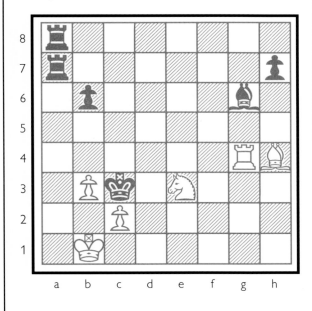

Nd1+
Nd5+

–4–
SCHOLAR'S MATE

THIS is a way to get checkmated in as little as four moves – and I'm sure none of our Bronze level trainees will allow that to happen to *them*.

The attack begins

1	e4	e5
2	Bc4	Bc5
3	Qh5	

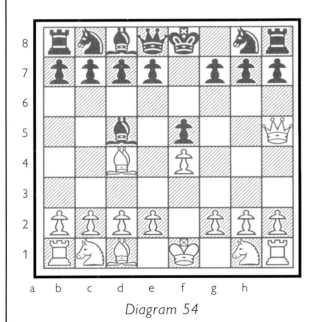

Diagram 54

White is threating checkmate – already! (by Q×f7). There are three ways to defend against it.

(1) **3. . . g6**

This is bad. It avoids checkmate, but still loses a rook.

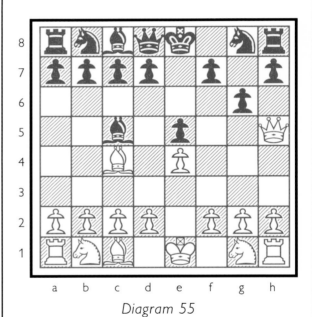

Diagram 55

4	Q×e5+!	Qe7
5	Q×h8	

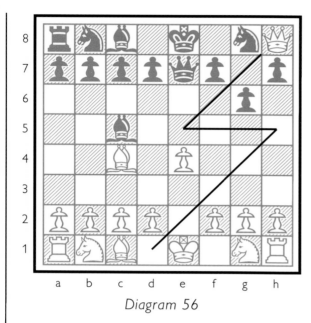

Diagram 56

White has won a rook using the zig-zag attack.

(2)   **3 ...**   **Nh6**

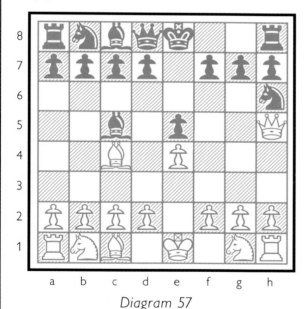

Diagram 57

This stops the mate, but loses a piece by a discovered attack.

    4   **d4!**   **B×d4**
    5   **B×h6!**

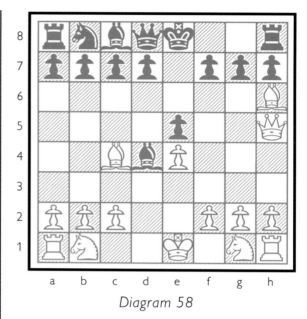

Diagram 58

Now if Black replies 5....g×h6, White plays 6 Q×f7++. If he doesn't, White stays a piece up.

(3)   **3 ... (Qf6 or Qe7)**

This is the best defence, guarding both e5 and f7.

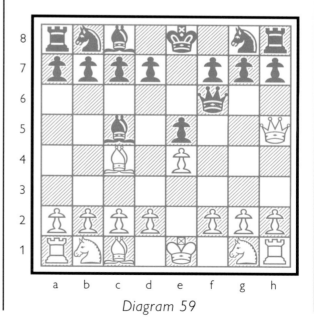

Diagram 59

If White now captures at f7, material is lost after 4 Q×f7+ Q×f7 5 B×f7+ K×f7. White is two capture points down.

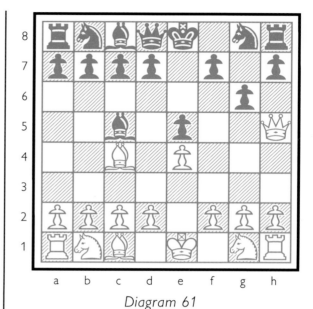

Diagram 61

What would you play for White here?

Questions on Scholar's Mate

Score 5 points for each answer. The answers are at the back of the book.

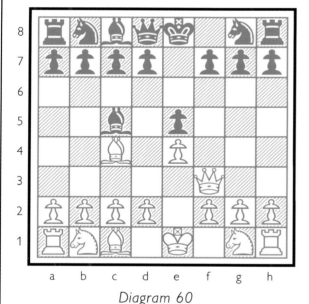

Diagram 60

What is White threatening?

Diagram 62

Why is Black's defence 3 ... Nh6 bad?

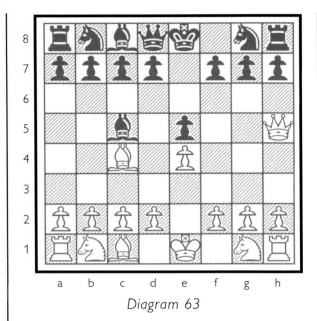

Diagram 63

What would you play as Black here?

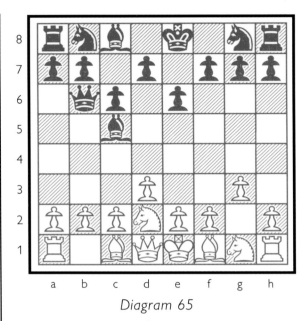

Diagram 65

Black to play; what is the best move?

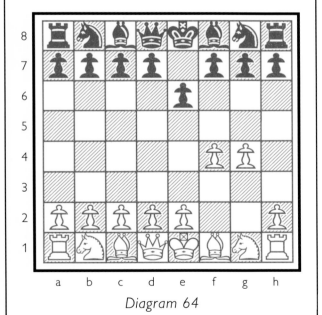

Diagram 64

What would you play as Black here?

–5–
THE SPECIAL RULES
CASTLING, STALEMATE, EN PASSANT

Castling

CASTLING is a double move of the king and rook, which can occur if there are no pieces between the king and the rook.

The rule is 'the king moves two spaces to the side, and the rook jumps over and stands alongside.'

You can castle either side of the board, and the diagrams show the pieces before and after castling; White castles on the kingside, and Black castles on the queenside.

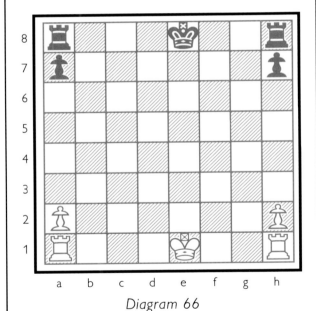

Diagram 66

There are certain cases when you cannot castle.

(1) You cannot castle if your king has already moved.

(2) If one of your rooks has moved, you cannot castle that side of the board; if both the rooks have moved, you cannot castle either side of the board.

(3) You cannot castle if your king is in check; but if you meet the check, without having to move your king, you can castle on future moves.

(4) You cannot castle *through* check (that is, your king must not pass over a square attacked by an enemy piece); and you cannot castle *into* check.

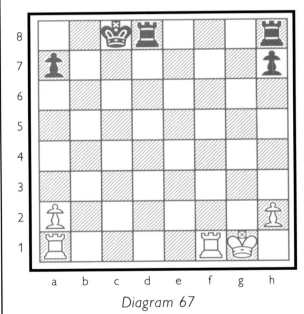

Diagram 67

You now know *how* to castle. But why *do* you castle? In the opening the king is a very weak piece, and it is in great danger. By castling, you tuck your king away in bed and put a blanket of pawns over him. Beware of pulling the blankets off him (by moving the pawns), as he may die of cold!

Examples

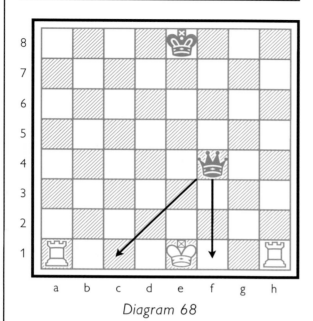

Diagram 68

In diagram 68, can White castle either side?

No. If the king goes to the kingside, it would be castling through check. If White tries castling queenside, the king would land in check on cl.

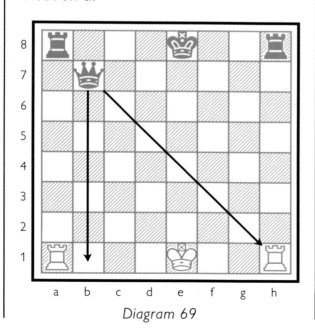

Diagram 69

In diagram 69, can White castle either side?

Yes. White can castle *both* kingside or queenside

The black queen is not attacking any squares that White will move the king over or on to during castling.

Important note: when you want to castle, you should touch your king first, not your rook. If you touch the rook, your opponent may insist that you move only the rook, and not castle.

Stalemate and other types of draws

When stalemate occurs, the game is drawn, even if one side is many pieces ahead.

If one player has the move, and that player's king is *not* in check, but any move that the player makes will put the king in check, and none of the player's other men can move, that is stalemate.

An example of stalemate:

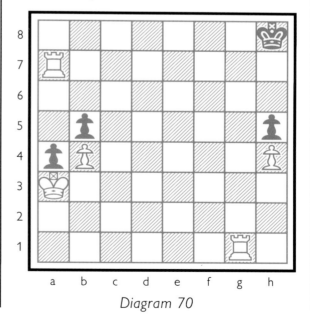

Diagram 70

Other types of drawn games

(1) Only two kings left on the board

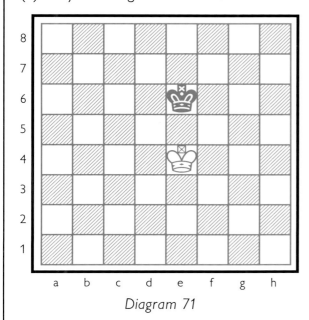

Diagram 71

(2) Perpetual check

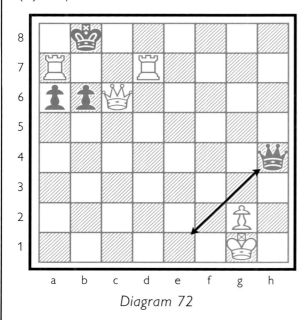

Diagram 72

1 ...   Qe1+
2 Kh2   Qh4+

3 Kg1   Qe1+   etc.

Black just keeps checking with the queen between h4 and e1.
(3) Position repeated three times (this can only be claimed if the game has been written down.
(4) Game drawn by agreement between the players.
(5) Not enough pieces left to mate with

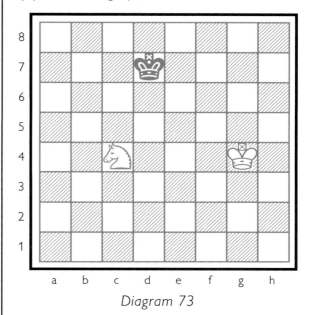

Diagram 73

King and knight versus king is drawn.

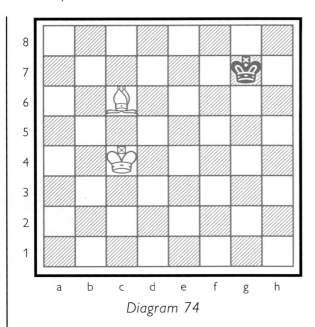

Diagram 74

King and bishop versus king is drawn.

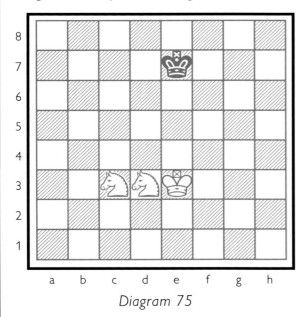

Diagram 75

King and two knights versus king is also drawn (mate cannot be forced).

But king and two bishops versus king, and king, bishop and knight versus king can be won with good play.

En passant – a type of pawn capture

If a pawn moves forward two squares to stand alongside an enemy pawn, this pawn can capture the pawn that has just moved *as though* it had only moved one square forward.

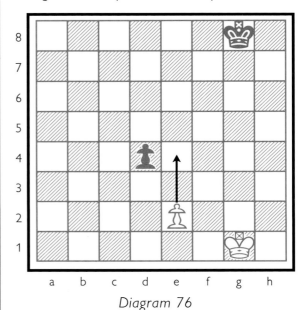

Diagram 76

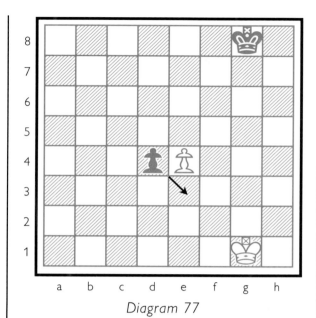

Diagram 77

White has just played e4. Black can now capture by dxe3 (see diagram 78).

The move would be written dxe3 e.p. (e.p. is short for en passant).

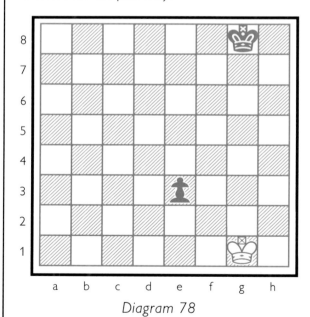

Diagram 78

The capture has to be made immediately if you want to make it; if Black had delayed a move, the right to make the capture would have been lost.

Tests on the special rules

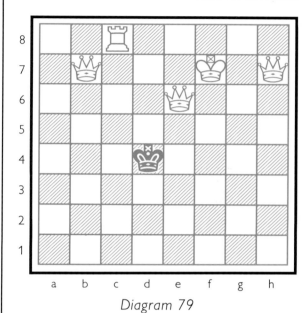

Diagram 79

Is this stalemate?

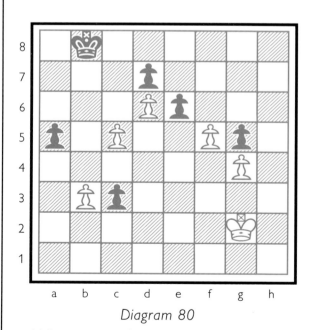

Diagram 80

White can make an en passant capture here; write the correct move.

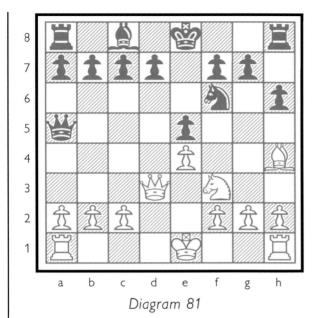

Diagram 81

Can White castle?

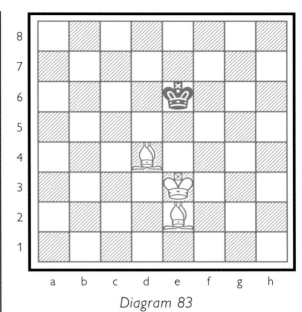

Diagram 83

Can White win in this position?

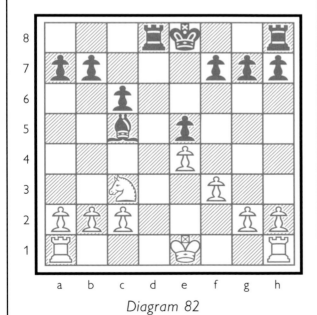

Diagram 82

White cannot castle; why not?

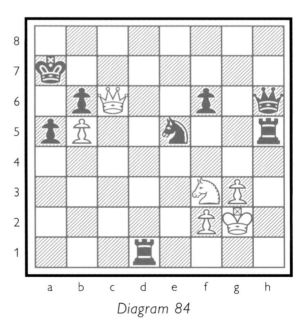

Diagram 84

White is two rooks down here. How can he draw?

–6–
THE BASIC MATES

The lawn mower

MATING with two rooks against a king

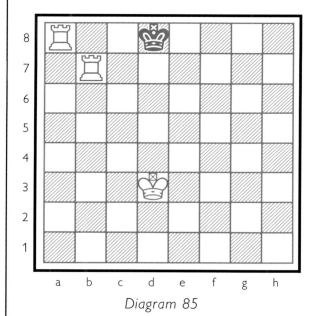

Diagram 85

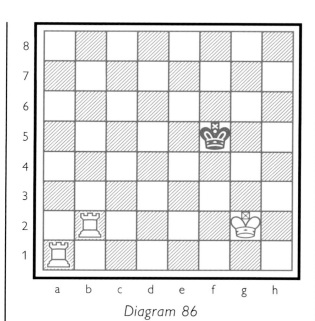

Diagram 86

1   Ra4

White builds a fence with one rook.

1   ....   Ke5
2   Rb5+

The other rook checks and forces the king to the edge of the board.

2   ....   Kd6
3   Ra6+

Now the *other* rook checks, while its companion holds the fence.

3   ....   Kc7

Now White cannot continue checking by Rb7+, because Black will capture the rook. In these positions, *move your rooks over to the other side of the board* and start checking again.

This is the sort of checkmate position you are aiming at. The enemy king is trapped on the edge by one rook, while the other gives checkmate.

Example – diagram 86 (play this out on your chess board):

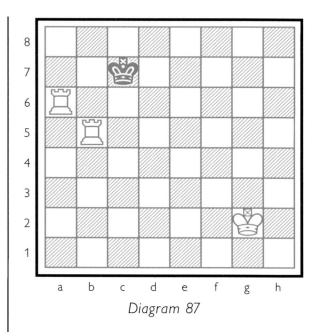

Diagram 87

4	**Rh6!**	**Kd7**
5	**Rb7+**	**Kc8**
6	**Rg7**	**Kd8**
7	**Rh8++**	

Voila!

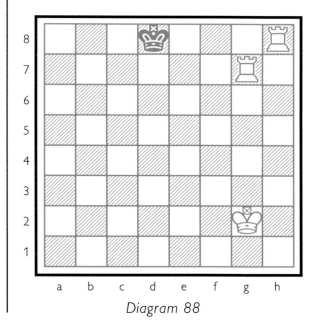

Diagram 88

Test

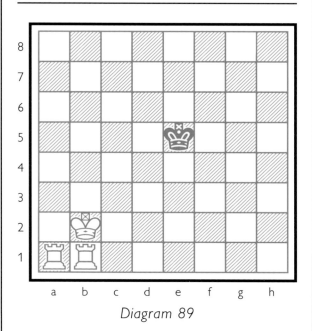

Diagram 89

Set up the position in diagram 89 and play it out against a friend or a computer, recording each move. The maximum number of moves allowed to give mate is 10. Score 24 points for checkmating. Add 2 bonus points for each move less than 10. (For example, if you checkmate in only 7 moves, give yourself 6 extra points.) The maximum bonus is 6 points.

The queen mate

This needs teamwork by the king and queen. Here are two examples of mate.

In both cases, the checkmated king is on the edge of the board.

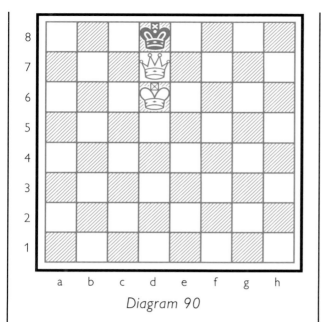

Diagram 90

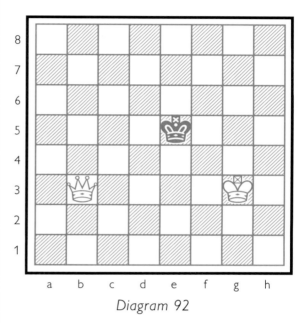

Diagram 92

Example (play this out on your chess board):

1   Qb6

Cuts the king off and forces it *towards* the white king.

1   ....   Kd5

Black must try to stay in the centre to try to stave off mate.

2   Kf4

Cutting off the king from the other side.

2   ....   Kc4
3   Ke4

Now the black king is squeezed towards the edge.

3   ....   Kc3

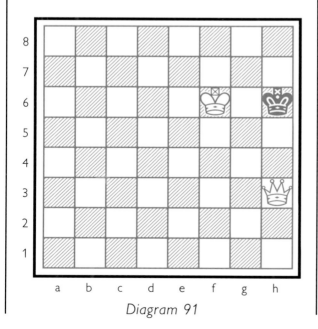

Diagram 91

Black's only move

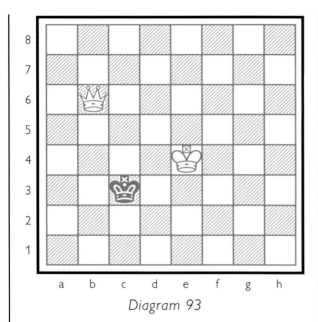

Diagram 93

4 Qb5

Stops the king returning to c4.

    4 ....   **Kc2**
    5 Qb4

Now the black king must go to the edge.

    5 ....   **Kd1**

Diagram 94

    6 Qb2!

An important rule: when the king is on the edge, trap him there by playing your queen one row off the edge. This avoids the danger of stalemate.

    6 ....   **Ke1**
    7 Ke3   **Kf1**
    8 Qf2++

The danger of stalemate

The queen is so powerful, it is easy for her to stalemate on her own.

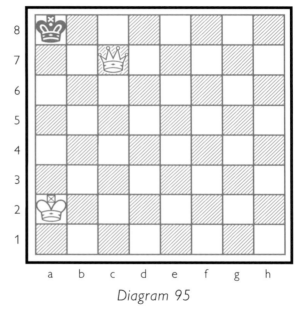

Diagram 95

Black to play is stalemated.

Another dangerous time is when the king and queen are about to deliver checkmate.

In diagram 96, the moves Kf4, Kf3, Kf2 all stalemate Black.

Remember the rule: when the enemy king is on the edge, *place your own queen one row off the edge to avoid stalemate.*

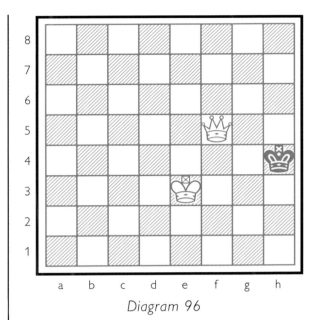

Diagram 96

1	Qg6!	Kh3
2	Kf3	Kh2
3	Qg2++	

A little care at the end ensures the win.

Test

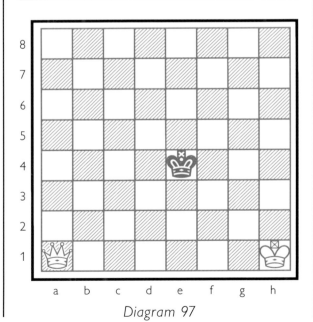

Diagram 97

Set up the position in diagram 97 on your chess board, and try to checkmate against a friend or a computer. Record all the moves.

The maximum number of moves allowed is 15. Score 36 points for this mate. Add 1 bonus point for every move you take less than 15. The maximum bonus is 8 points.

The 'box mate'

The mate with the king and rook against king is harder, but you need the same teamwork by the white pieces to drive the king to the edge.

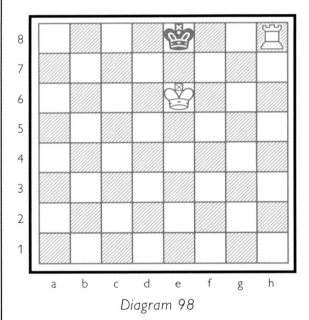

Diagram 98

Here is the mating pattern: the rook checks from the side, and the king prevents the enemy king from escaping.

There are three stages in this mate:

(1) Make a box with the king and the rook, and trap the enemy king inside it.

(2) Make the box smaller and smaller, forcing the king to the edge of the board.

(3) Checkmate.

Example (play this out on your chess board):

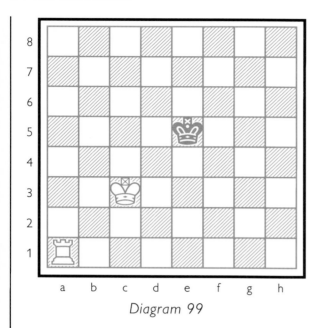

Diagram 99

1	Ra4	Kd5
2	Rd4+	Ke5

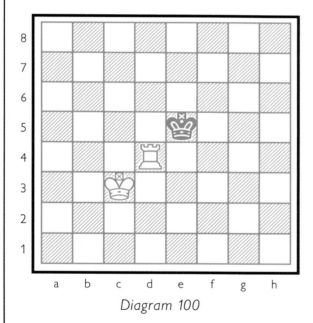

Diagram 100

The box is watertight; the rook, protected by the white king, holds the enemy king in a small area of 16 squares. Now to make the box smaller.

3	Kc4	Ke6
4	Rd5	

Black has only 12 squares now.

4	....	Kf6
5	Kd4	Ke6
6	Ke4	Ke7
7	Ke5	Kf7
8	Rd6	Ke7

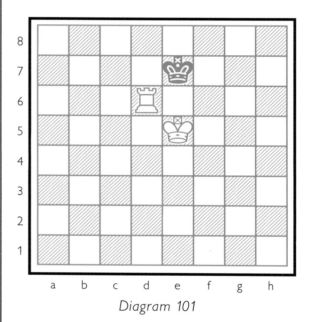

Diagram 101

Black has 8 squares now, but White cannot make any progress and must make a *waiting move* with the king. Whatever you do, don't make the box larger.

9	Kd5	Kf7

Black has to give way.

10	Re6	Kg7
11	Ke5	Kf7
12	Kf5	Kg7
13	Rf6	

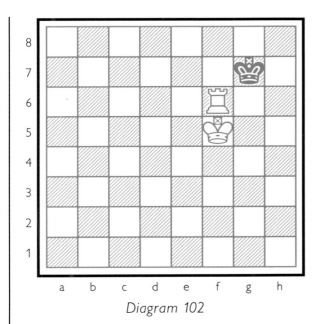

Diagram 102

Four squares left now.

13 .... Kh8

14 Kg6

The black king is on the edge, and White comes in for the kill.

14 .... Kg8

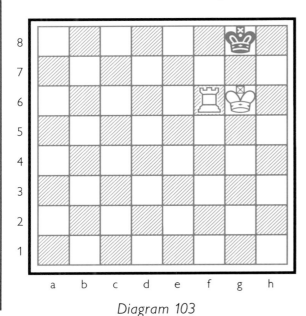

Diagram 103

This is the tricky bit. Here a waiting move with the rook is the best idea.

15 Rf1!! Kh8

Black has no other move.

16 Rf8++

___

Test

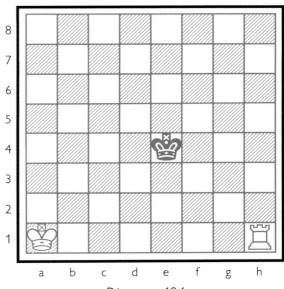

Diagram 104

Set up the position of diagram 104, and try to checkmate against a friend or a computer. Record all the moves.

You score 40 points for this mate. Add a bonus of 1 point for each move under 25 taken to deliver the mate. The maximum number of moves allowed is 25, and the maximum number of bonus points is 10. Maximum score for this mate = 50.

–7–
DEFEND YOURSELF!

WHEN one of your men is under attack, you can move it, capture the attacker, support the attacked man, or block the attack. Move, Capture, Support, Block, or MCSB for short.

In these exercises, one of your men is attacked. Show all the good ways to defend against the threat. *Any move that does not lose material points is good.*

Example 1

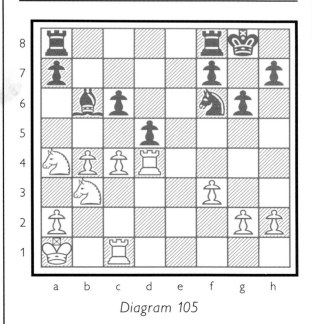

Diagram 105

Here the rook at d4 is attacked. If we allow the bishop at b6 to capture, we will lose at least 2 capture points, even if we recapture. Our good defences are:

MOVE: Rd3, Rd2, Rddl, Rf4, Rh4
BLOCK: c5, Nac5, Nbc5
CAPTURE: Nxb6

It is not good to support the rook, as it is *more valuable* than the attacking bishop.

Moves like Re4 and Rg4 are also not good, because the rook can be captured on that square.

Example 2

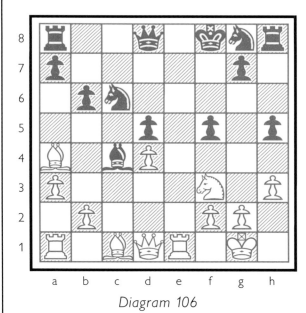

Diagram 106

The knight at c6 is attacked. Good defences are:

MOVE: Na5, Nb8, Nce7
SUPPORT: Rc8, Nge7, Qc8, Qc7, Qd7,

Qd6, Qf6,
BLOCK: b5

There are eleven good defensive moves; seven of them are supports, as we don't mind swapping a bishop for a knight.

Practice exercise

In diagrams 107 and 108, find all the good defensive moves against the attack, using MCSB.

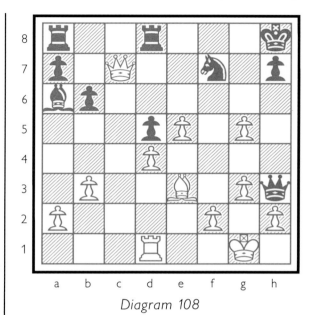

Diagram 108

The black knight at f7 is attacked by the queen at c7.

The answers are on the next page.

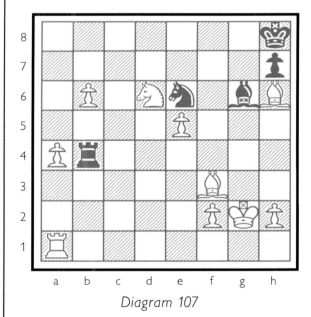

Diagram 107

The white pawn at b6 is attacked by the rook at b4.

Test

Score 2 points for each good defensive move found. Deduct 2 points for each bad defensive move written down (moves that lose capture points). Add 1 bonus point for each minute less than 25 you took to solve the test. The maximum bonus is 12 points. (Maximum total score = 68. The answers are at the end of the book.

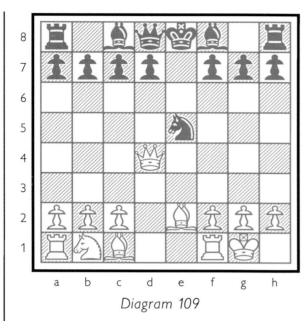

Diagram 109

The black knight on e5 is attacked by the white queen on d4.

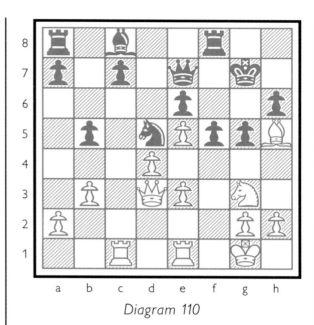

Diagram 110

The black pawn on b5 is attacked by the white queen on d3.

Answers to diagrams 107 and 108

Diagram 107:

MOVE	:	b7
CAPTURE	:	–
SUPPORT	:	a5, Nc8, Be3
BLOCK	:	Nb5

Diagram 108:

MOVE	:	–
CAPTURE	:	–
SUPPORT	:	Kg8, Kg7, Rf8, Qe6, Qf5, Qh5
BLOCK	:	Rd7, Qd7

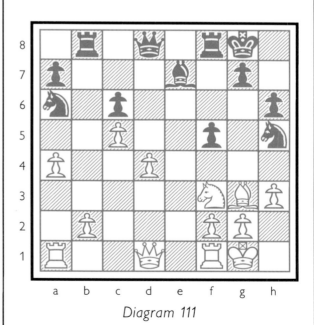

Diagram 111

The black rook on b8 is attacked by the white bishop on g3.

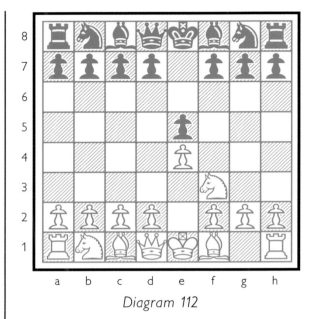

Diagram 112

The black pawn on e5 is attacked by the white knight on f3.

-8-
NOW YOU PLAY!

ONE of the things you quickly notice about playing chess is how easy it is to make mistakes. Basic mistakes are of two types:

(1) Placing errors. You place a piece where it can be captured for nothing, or lose it in exchange for a less valuable piece.

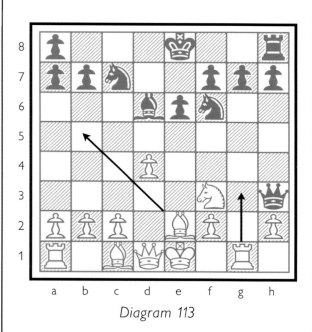

Diagram 113

Here Bb5+ is a placing error; Black can capture it for nothing by N×b5.

Another placing error would be Rg3; after the capture and recapture B×g3 h×g3, White is two points down.

(2) Missing a direct attack. In diagram 14 Black's last move made a direct attack on the white queen by Rg6. If White ignores this and plays, say, Nc3, he commits a basic error.

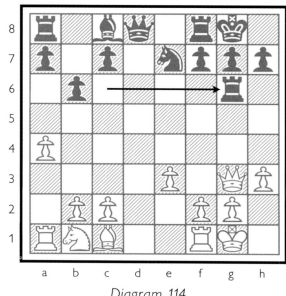

Diagram 114

In order to pass this course, you need to be able to play at least two games of 20 moves without making any basic errors.

To help you do this, I have devised a thinking routine to ensure that all your games are of this high standard.

You should record all your important games, and it is a good idea to use a pencil and rubber for recording, rather than a pen.

Here is the routine:

(1) Choose your move in your head, but don't touch the piece.

(2) Write the move down.

(3) *Look* at the square you intend to put your piece on and ask yourself: 'is it safe?'.

(4) If it is not safe and you are going to lose

capture points by making the move, rub it out (or cross it out if you are writing in pen) and go back to stage 1.

(5) If the move is 'safe', place a tick after it on your score sheet.

(6) Play the move

Now wait for your opponent to reply. When this move has been made:

(7) Write the move down.

(8) Check to see if it is a blunder and you can win capture points. Check to see if it threatens to capture one of your men.

(9) If there is no threat, put a dash after the move on the score sheet and go back to stage 1.

(10) If there is a threat, place a triangle sign after the move. You can use your MCSB routines to decide on your answer. Then go back to stage 1.

Here is how a game would look, recorded using ticks and triangles method.

1	e4	✓	d5	▲
2	e×d5	✓	Q×d5	—
3	Nc3	✓	Qa5	—
4	d4	✓	Nf6	—
5	Bc4	✓	Bg4	▲
6	Qd3	✓	e6	—

Here is a description of what might have been going on in White's head while making these moves.

'I think I'll play pawn to e4. It releases two of my pieces for action, the queen and the bishop.' *(Writes the move down.)* 'Is the square safe?' Yes. *(Ticks the move and plays it.)* 'He's moved his pawn to d5.' *(Writes the move down.)*

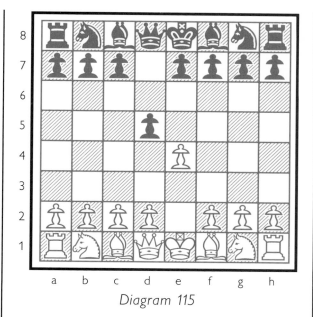

Diagram 115

'Can I win a pawn here by e×d5? No, it's defended by his queen. Is he threatening me? Yes, he wants to take my pawn at e4.' *(Puts a triangle after the move d5.)* 'Let's see — Move, capture, support, block — I think I'll capture this time.' *(Writes down the move e×d5.)* 'Is it safe? Yes, he can recapture the pawn, but swaps don't lose me any material.' *(Ticks the move and plays it.)* 'Now he's played Q×d5.'

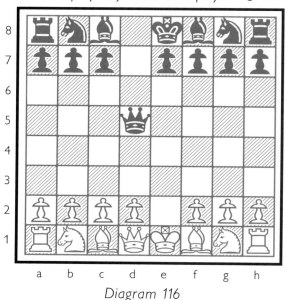

Diagram 116

(Writes this down.)

'Can I take his queen? No. Is the queen threatening any of my pieces? It's attacking three of my pawns at a2, d2 and g2, but they're all defended, so that's all right.' *(Places a dash after the move Qxd5.)*

'What shall I play? Why not bring out my knight attacking his queen? That looks like a good move.' *(Writes it down.)* 'Is the square c3 safe? Yes.' *(Ticks the move and then plays it. The opponent moves his queen to a5. Writes this move down.)*

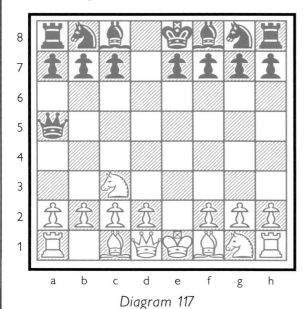

Diagram 117

'Can I take on a5 with any of my pieces? Pity. But never mind, he's not threatening me either. Well, he is attacking my knight now, but that's defended twice.' *(Puts a dash after the move Qa5.)*

'Now it's my turn. What about attacking his queen again with pawn to b4? That's a good idea.' *(Writes the move down.)* 'I'd better check this. Is it safe? Of course not; he can take it by Qxb4.' *(Rubs the move out.)* 'I'll choose something else. What about pawn to d4? That puts a pawn in the centre, and releases my bishop at c1 for action.' *(Writes the move down.)* 'The move looks safe' *(Ticks the move on the score sheet and plays it.)* 'Now he's brought his knight to f6.' *(Writes the*

move down.) 'He's playing very quickly, but I mustn't let that disturb me. Can I take his knight on f6? No, I've got nothing attacking that square. Is the knight threatening me? No.' *(Places a dash after the move.)* 'That leaves me free to choose my next move. I think I'll bring my bishop out on to a central square at c4. It's much more active there than back at f1.' *(Writes the move down.)* 'Now to check if the square is safe. Yes, there's nothing attacking c4.' *(Ticks the move Bc4 and plays it. The opponent moves Bg4.)*

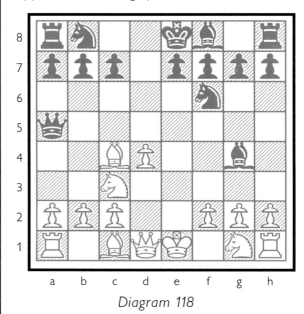

Diagram 118

'What's this? He's attacking my queen, but he's blundered his bishop away.' *(Hurriedly writes the move down and puts a triangle after it.)* 'I can take it with my queen and I'll be three points up! Yippee!' *(Writes down Qxg4.)* 'But I'd better check the move first. Wait a minute. He can take my queen on g4 with his knight. Help!' *(Rubs the move out.)* 'Phew. Thank goodness for ticks and triangles. That could have cost me my queen! I think I'll use MCSB to get out of this one. I certainly can't capture the bishop, and it's no use supporting my queen, but I can use block or move. I think I'll move my queen up to d3.' *(Writes the move down.)* 'Is it safe? Yes.' *(Ticks the move and plays it.)* 'He's played pawn to e6.' *(Writes the move down and the game continues. . . .)*

If you can think as well as this young player did, you are certain to complete the course successfully.

Test

Play several recorded games, using the ticks and triangles method. The games should last at least 20 moves, so you will probably need an hour to play in.

Here is a brief summary of the ticks and triangles routine:

(1) Choose your move
(2) Write it down
(3) Check 'Is it safe?'
(4) No. Rub out the move; go back to stage 1
(5) Yes. Tick ✓
(6) Play
Opponent moves
(7) Write it down
(8) Is it a blunder?
Is there a threat?
(9) No threat. Put a dash —and go back to stage 1.
(10) Threat. Put a ▲ sign, use MCSB and go back to stage 1.

Some general advice

Besides making sure you are not making any basic errors, what else should you be thinking about when you are choosing your moves? You should be trying to place your pieces where they attack more squares, and trying to attack enemy pieces. It is useful to get a pawn in the centre in the beginning of the game, and to castle your king into safety early on.

-9-
THE FINAL TEST

NOW that you have worked your way through the course this far, you should be ready to take the Final Test. This will test you on all that you have learned so far, so make sure that you revise all of the chapters, particularly those on Scholar's Mate and the special rules.

When you have completed the Final Test, you need to do two things. First, you should check your answers against those given at the end of the book, and add up the number of points that you have scored. If you score 75 percent or higher, then you are half-way to success.

The second step is to play at least two games of no less than 20 moves each, without making a basic error in either game. (Basic errors are described on page 36.) Remember that you don't have to win these games; just make sure that you have made no basic errors in them. Ask your chess teacher or a strong player to check this.

Provided that you scored at least 75 percent on the Final Test, and that you have played two games without basic errors, you have passed the course, and can now go on to play competitive chess with confidence. But don't worry if you didn't quite make it at the first attempt. Just go back and study the parts of the book that caused you trouble in the Final Test, and when you are sure that you understand them, take the test again.

NB

There is no time limit on the Final Test, but you should attempt all of the questions on one sitting, if possible.

Answer all the questions. Write your answers on a separate sheet of paper.

1

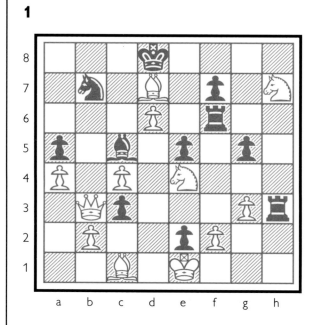

Write down all the captures White could make on this move.

2

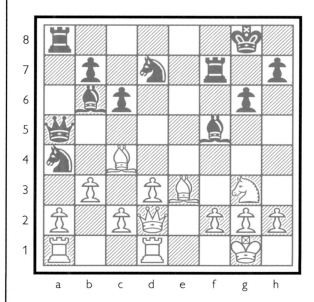

(a) Write down the moves by White which exchange material.

(b) Write down the moves by White which gain material.

3

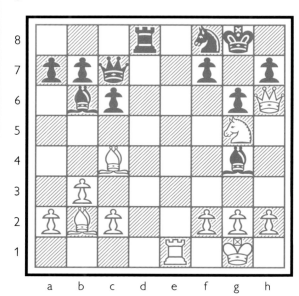

Write down a move which checkmates Black.

4

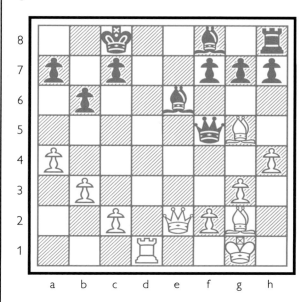

Write down a move which checkmates Black.

5

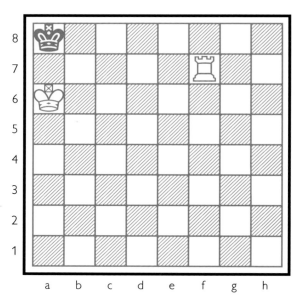

(a) Write down a move that checkmates Black.

(b) Write down a move that stalemates Black.

6

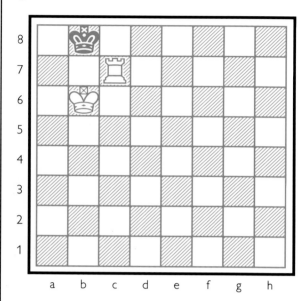

White to play. Write down a move that forces checkmate in two moves.

8

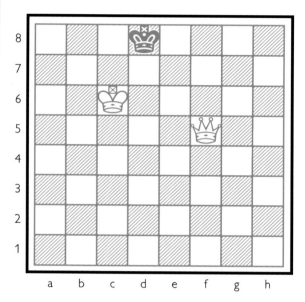

(a) Write down *two* moves that mate.
(b) Write down a move that stalemates.

7

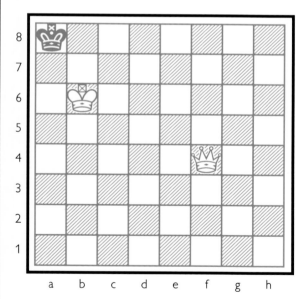

(a) Write down a move that checkmates Black.
(b) Write down a move that stalemates Black.

9

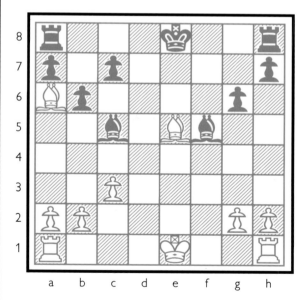

(a) Can White castle kingside?
(b) Can White castle queenside?
(c) Can Black castle kingside?
(d) Can Black castle queenside?

10

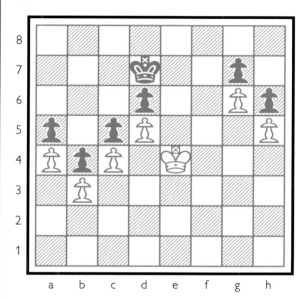

White can capture en passant in this position.

(a) What was Black's last move?

(b) Write down White's en passant capture.

11

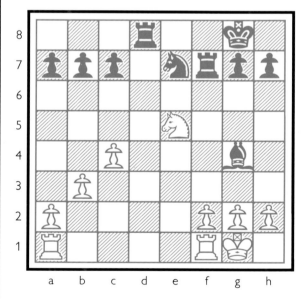

(a) Which pieces does White's knight

attack?

(b) What move should White play?

12

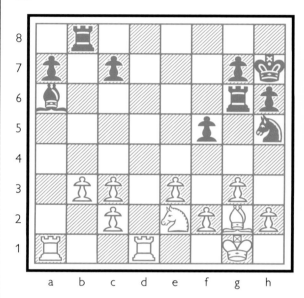

Black has just played Ba6. Write down all White's good defences, using MCSB.

13

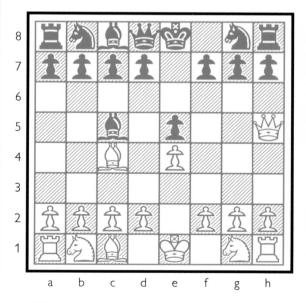

(a) What would you play here as Black?

(b) Why did you do this?

14

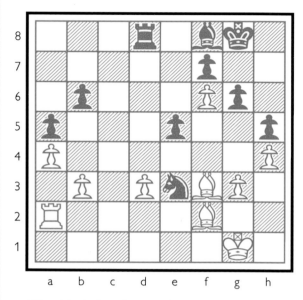

The black knight at e3 is attacked. Using MCSB, write down all the good defensive moves.

16

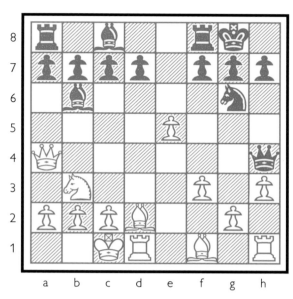

Black has just played Qh4. What would you now play as White?

15

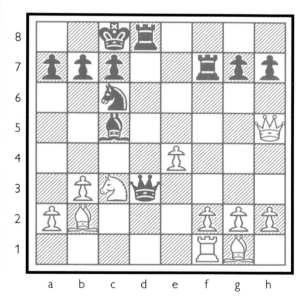

(a) What pieces does the white queen attack?
(b) What capture should White make?

17

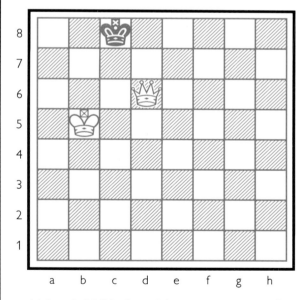

What is White's quickest way to mate?

18

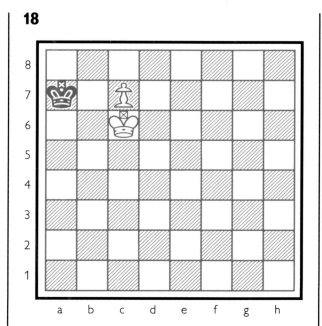

White to play and mate in two moves.

–10–
SUPPLEMENTARY EXERCISES

THIS test will give you extra practice in many of the important subjects in this book.

Supplementary exercises 1: writing moves

Write down the moves as shown by the arrows in the diagrams. Score 2 points for each move correctly written.

Par time: 20 minutes. Add 1 bonus point for each minute below 20. Maximum bonus = 12. Maximum total score = 60.

1

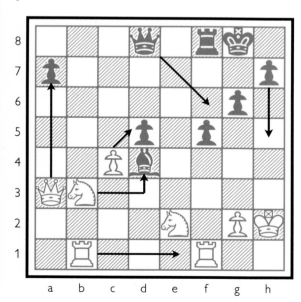

2

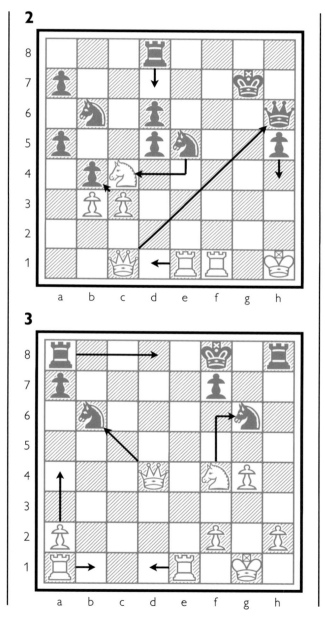

3

4

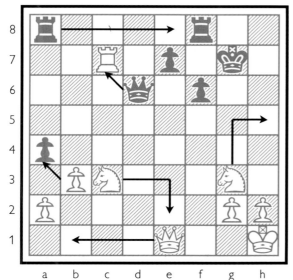

1

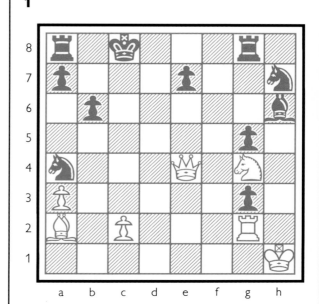

Supplementary test 2: seeing captures

Write down all the captures you can see for *White* on this move.

Score 1 point for each capture found. Par time: 25 minutes. Time bonus: Add 1 bonus point for each minute below 25. Maximum time bonus = 10. Maximum score = 40.

2

3

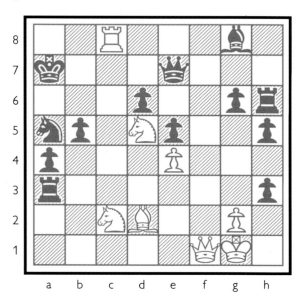

Supplementary test 3: value of the pieces

Write down all the captures you can see for *White* in these diagrams, and put in brackets after each capture the number of capture points gained.

Score 1 point for each capture.

Par time: 25 minutes. Time bonus: Add 1 bonus point for each minute below 25. Maximum time bonus = 7. Maximum score = 40.

1

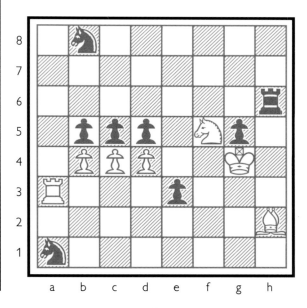

4

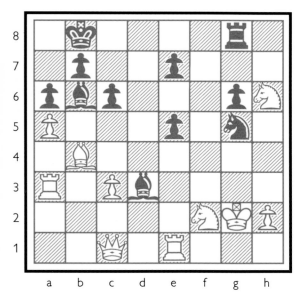

2

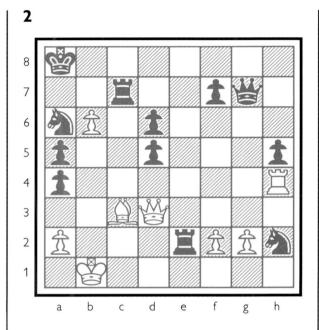

4

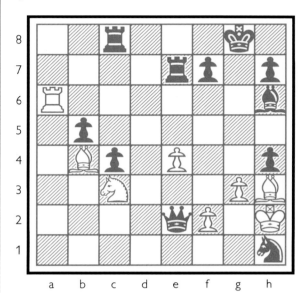

3

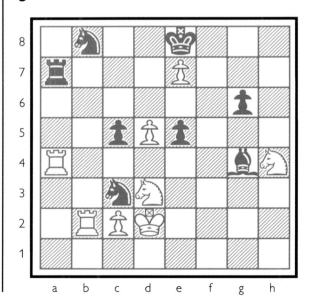

Supplementary test 4: capture and recapture (1)

Write down all the captures and recaptures that GAIN and EXCHANGE material for White. Put in brackets the number of points gained as a result. If you have simply swapped pieces, put a zero in brackets. If there is no recapture, simply put the number of points gained in brackets after the move.

Score 2 points for each correct answer. Deduct 3 points if you wrote down a move that loses capture points.

Par time: 30 minutes. Add 1 bonus point for each minute below 30. Maximum time bonus = 10. Maximum score = 50.

1

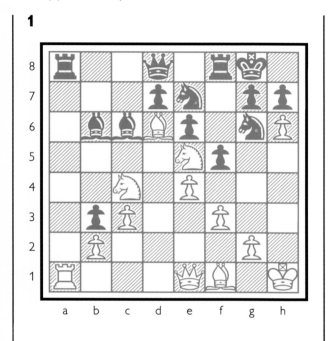

2

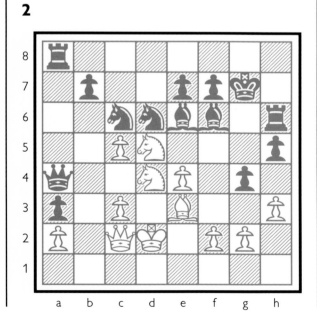

3

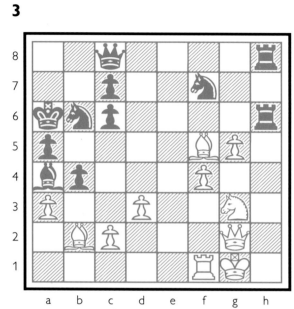

4

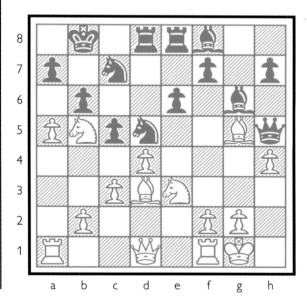

Supplementary test 5: capture and recapture (2)

Write down all the captures and recaptures that GAIN and EXCHANGE material for White. Put in brackets the number of points gained as a result. If you have simply swapped pieces, put a zero in brackets. If there is no recapture, simply put the number of points gained in brackets after the move.

Score 2 points for each correct answer. Deduct 3 points if you wrote down a move that loses capture points.

Par time: 30 minutes. Add 1 bonus point for each minute below 30. Maximum time bonus = 8. Maximum score = 50.

2

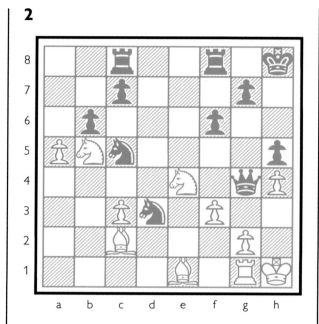

1

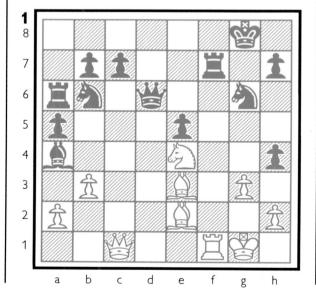

3

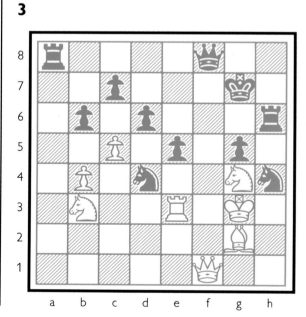

4

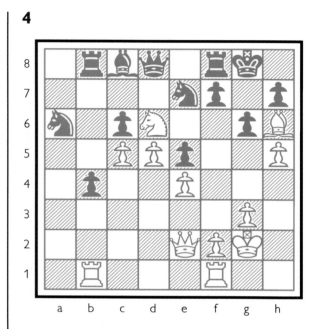

1

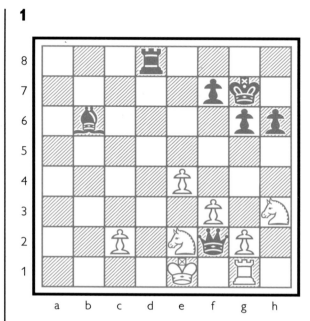

2

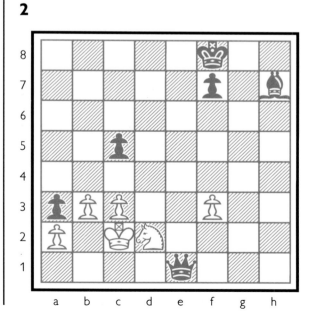

Supplementary exercises 6: getting out of check (1)

You are White. In each diagram, find the one move that gets you out of check.

Score 3 points for each correct defence.

Par time: 15 minutes. Add 1 bonus point for each minute below 15. Maximum bonus = 7. Maximum score = 25.

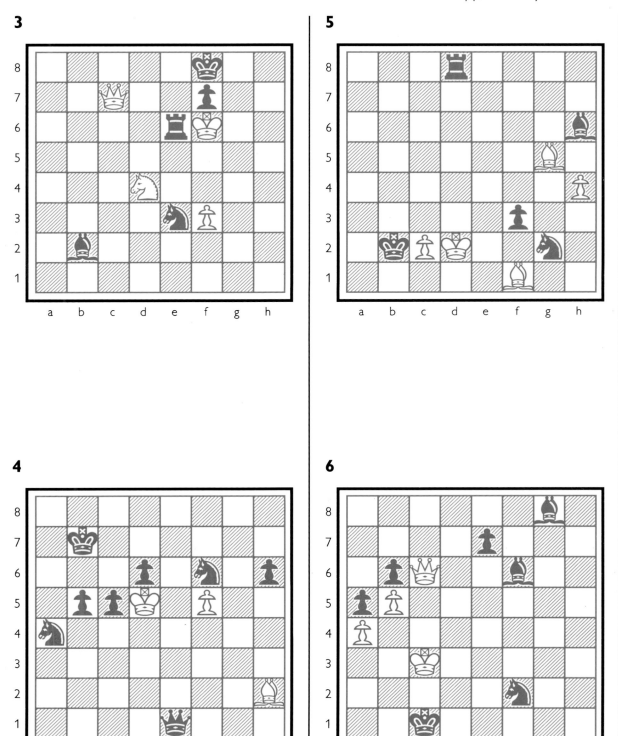

Supplementary exercises 7: getting out of check (2)

You are White. In each diagram find the one move to get you out of check. Score 3 points for each correct answer.

Par time: 15 minutes. Add 1 bonus point for each minute below 15. Maximum bonus = 7. Maximum score = 25.

2

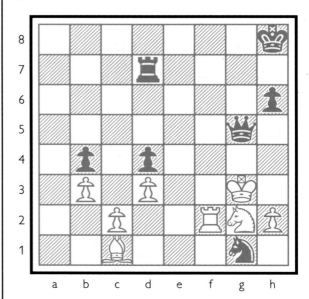

1

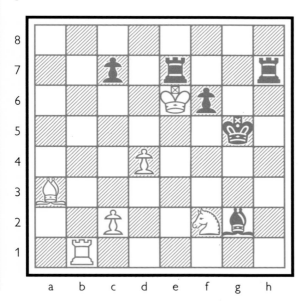

3

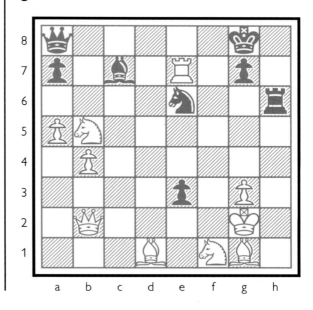

4

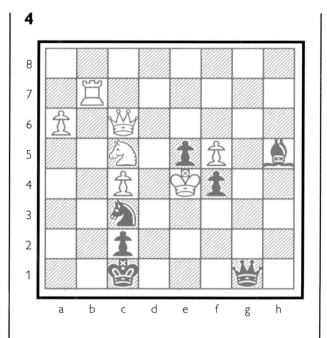

6

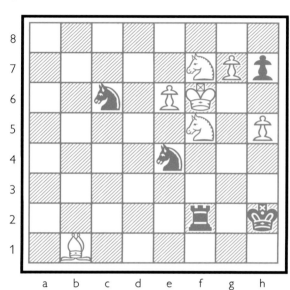

5

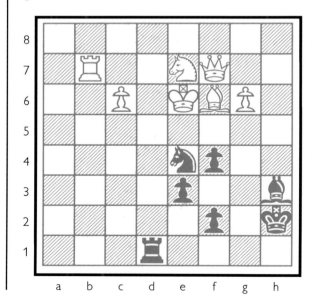

Supplementary exercises 8: checkmate (1)

You are White. In each diagram find the one move to checkmate Black. Score 6 points for each correct solution.

Par time: 25 minutes. Add 1 bonus point for each minute below 25. Maximum bonus = 14. Maximum score = 50.

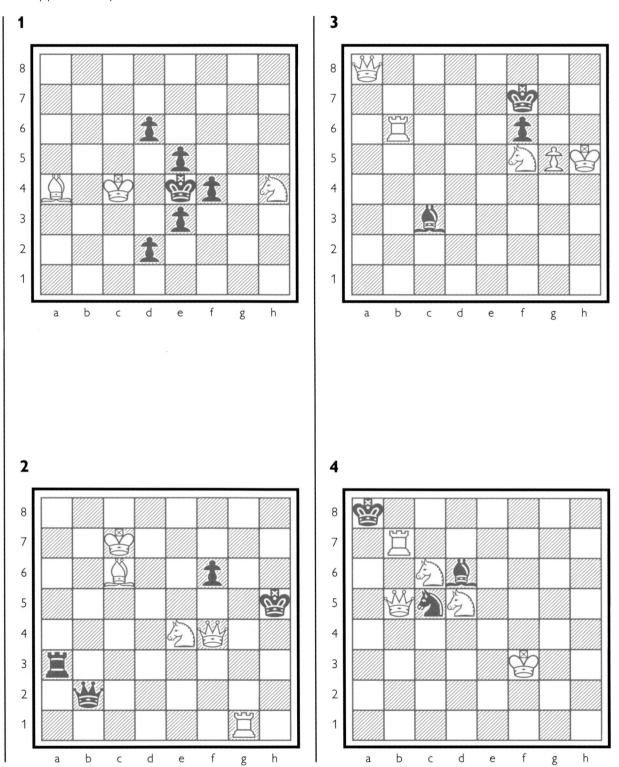

5

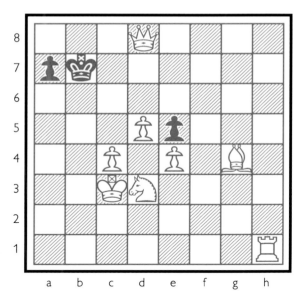

Supplementary exercises 9: checkmate (2)

You are White. In each diagram, find the one move to checkmate Black. Score 6 points for each correct solution.

Par time: 25 minutes. Add 1 bonus point for each minute below 25. Maximum bonus = 14. Maximum score = 50.

6

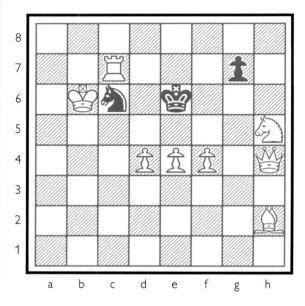

1

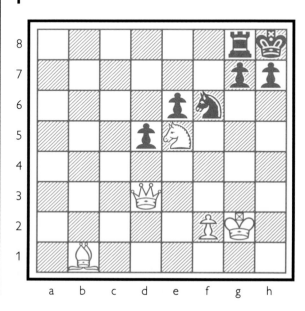

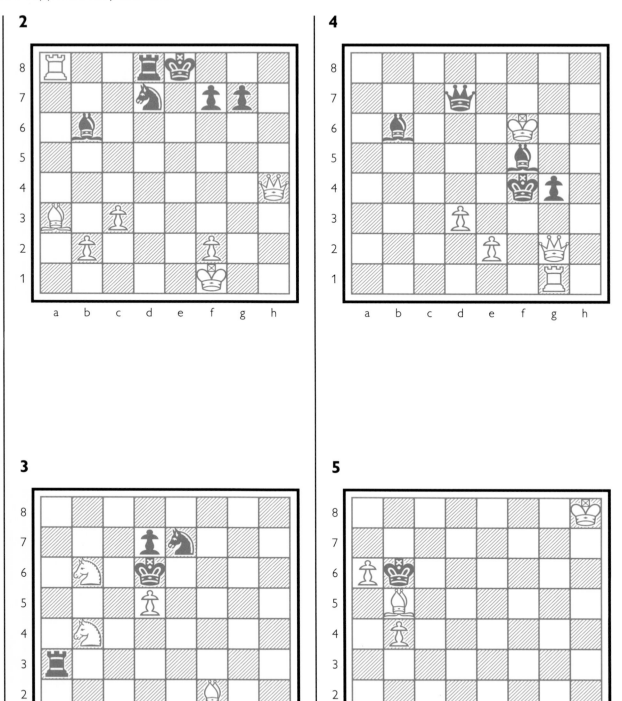

6

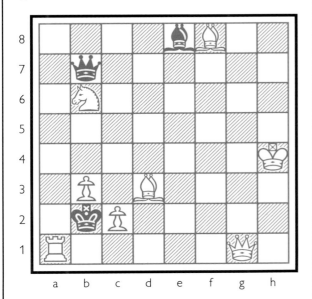

1

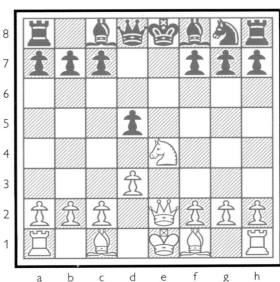

Supplementary exercises 10: harder checkmates in one move, involving pins, discoveries and double checks

You are White. In each diagram find the one move to checkmate Black. Score 6 points for each correct answer. Add 1 bonus point for each minute below 25. Maximum bonus = 14. Maximum score = 50.

2

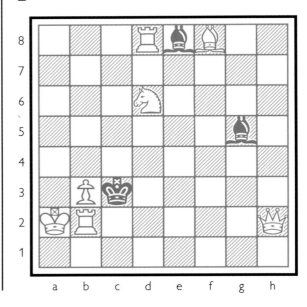

3

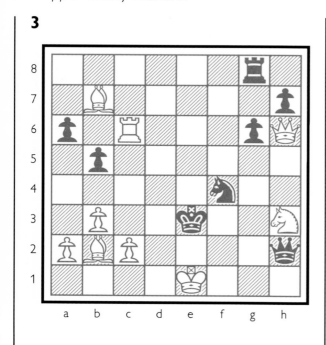

5

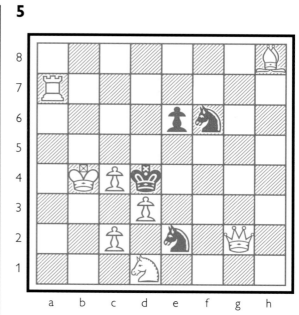

4

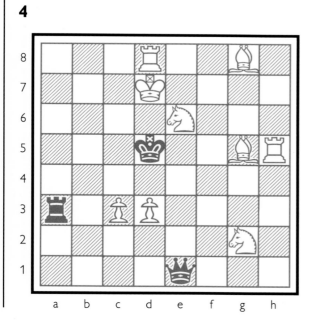

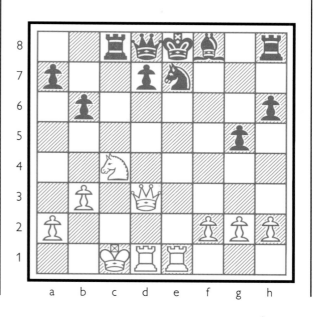

Supplementary test 11: MCSB (1)

Find all the good defences to the attacks in the diagrams, using MCSB (Move, Capture, Support, Block). Score 2 points for each good defensive move written down. Deduct 2 points for each bad defensive move written down (moves losing material).

Par time: 30 minutes. Add 1 bonus point for each minute below 30. Maximum bonus = 8 points. maximum score = 60 points.

2

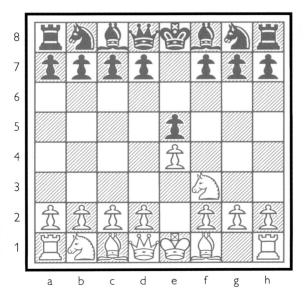

Pawn at e5 attacked

1

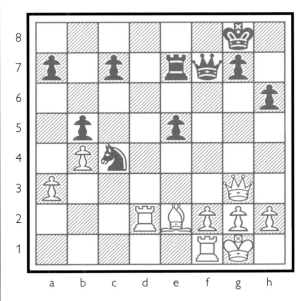

Rook at d2 attacked

3

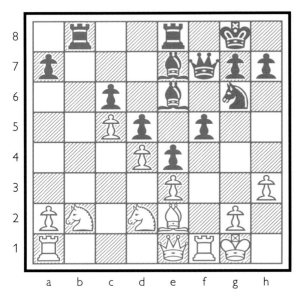

Knight at b2 attacked.

4

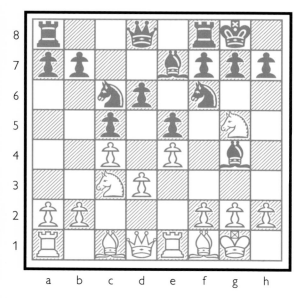

Queen at d1 attacked

1

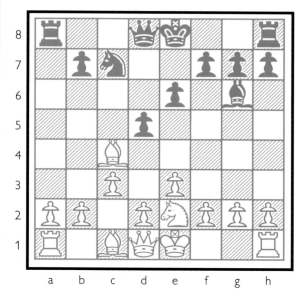

Bishop at c4 attacked

Supplementary test 12: MCSB (2)

Write down all the good defensive moves to the attacks in the diagrams, using MCSB. *Any move that does not lose capture points is good.* Score 2 points for each good move. Deduct 3 points for each bad defensive move.

Par time: 30 minutes. Add 1 bonus point for each minute below 30. Maximum bonus = 10. Maximum score = 70.

2

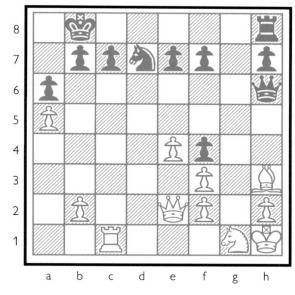

Knight at d7 attacked

3

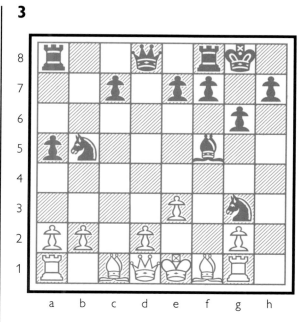

Knight at b5 attacked

4

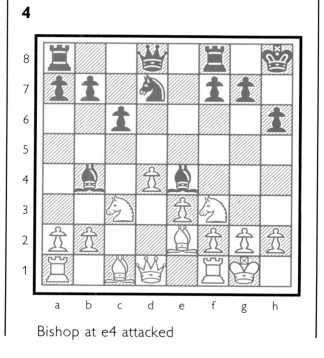

Bishop at e4 attacked

SUPPLEMENTARY TESTS SCORE CHART

	Score	bonus	total	Max
1 WRITING MOVES				60
2 SEEING CAPTURES				40
3 VALUE OF THE PIECES				40
4 CAPTURE AND RECAPTURE (1)				50
5 CAPTURE AND RECAPTURE (2)				50
6 GETTING OUT OF CHECK (1)				25
7 GETTING OUT OF CHECK (2)				25
8 CHECKMATE (1)				50
9 CHECKMATE (2)				50
10 HARDER CHECKMATES				50
11 MCSB (1)				60
12 MCSB (2)				70
Total				570
Percentage				

–II–
ANSWERS

Answers to tests

1. Writing moves (*Diagrams 9 – 12*)

Diagram 9	*Diagram 10*	*Diagram 11*	*Diagram 12*
Ba4	Nab5	Rc1	Rb×b6
	or N3b5		or R3×b6
Bd5	B×a8	Q×d7+	B×e5
Qg5	Re6	Rd8	Qh1
g4	d×e4	Bh6	R7f5
Nh5	Rbf1	Nh3	Kg8
Ra8	g4	Kf1	h5

2. Seeing captures (*Diagrams 14 and 15*)

Diagram 14	*Diagram 15*
N×a6	B×g7
N×d5	N×c7+
R×c7	Q×a6+
Q×a4	Q×f3
Q×h5	e×f5
B×e7	R×h4

3(i) Value of the pieces: Captures in order of value (*Diagrams 17 and 18*)

Diagram 17	*Diagram 18*
c×d4 (5)	R×c8 (9)
R×e2 (3)	h×g7 (5)
R×f8 (3)	B×g7 (5)
Q×b5 (3)	B×f4 (5)
Q×g8 (3)	R×a3+ (3)
B×b7 (1)	Q×a7+ (3)
R×a5 (1)	B×d5 (1)
	R×g6 (1)

3(ii) Capturing and recapturing (*Diagrams 20 – 23*)

Diagram 20

N×a8 B×a8 (+2)	Bad captures:
g×f5 g×f5 (+2)	B×b5 a×b5 (–2)
Q×h4 N×h4 (0)	Q×c3 d×c3 (–8)
b×c3 d×c3 (0)	N×a6 B×a6 (–2)
	N×b5 a×b5 (–2)

Diagram 21

R×b6 c×b6 (+4)	
N×d5 e×d5 (2+)	
B×h7+ N×h7 (0)	No bad captures possible
B×g5 N×g5 (0)	in this position!
h×g4 h×g4 (0)	
R×f6 B×f6 (0)	

Diagram 22

N×c7 R×c7 (+2)	
h×g4 h×g4 (+2)	Bad captures:
Q×h6 g×h6 (0)	N×c5 b×c5 (–2)
b×c5 b×c5 (0)	Q×d7 R×d7 (–6)
N×f6 N×f6 (0)	

Diagram 23

B×f8 Q×f8 (+2)	Bad captures:
g×f5 g×f5 (+2)	N×g6 h×g6 (–2)
Q×d8 R×d8 (0)	
N×c6 R×c6 (0)	
N×f3 g×f3 (0)	

4. Getting out of check (Diagrams 28 – 39)

28:	NXd2	34:	Kd7
29:	Ka4	35:	Kd4
30:	RXg8+	36:	Bd7
31:	Bc3	37:	Kd2
32:	g3	38:	Bf4
33:	Nd2	39:	BXg5

5. Checkmating (Diagrams 41 – 46)

41:	Qf7++	44:	Bh3++
42:	Rf6++	45:	Rg6++
43:	Ng7++	46:	Ne4++

(These are the *only* moves that checkmate)

6. Is it checkmate? (Diagrams 48 – 53)

48: Qf8++   49: Qc5++
   Nd5+   Ke6   Rdl+   Ke7 or Ke5
   Qb7+   Ke8 or Kd8   Ne4+   Ke5 or Kd5 or Ke7
   Rf7+   BXf7   Qd4+   Ke7
50: Qh6++
   Ng5+   Kg6 or RXg5 or Kh8
   Qc2+   f5 or Bf5 or Rg6 or Kh8 or Qe4
   Qd3+   Rg6 or f5 or Bf5 or Kh8 or Qe4
51: Na6++
   Qe5+   Kd7 or Nd6 or Kd8 or Kb6
   Rh7+   Kb8 or Ne7 or Kd6
   Qg7+   Kb8 or Kb6 or Kd8 or Ne7
52: Bel++   53: Qh6++
   Rc4+   Kd2   Bc3+   Kh7 or f6 or Kf8
   Nd5+   Kd2   Qd4+   Kh7 or f6 or Kf8
   Ndl+   Kd2   Rg6+   KXg6 or Kh8 or fXg6 or Kf8

7. Scholar's Mate (Diagrams 60 – 65)

60: QXf7++
61: QXe5+ and QXh8 winning a rook
62: White can play d4! followed by BXh6
63: Qf6 or Qe7 to defend f7 and e5
64: Qh4++
65: BXf2++

8. Special rules (Diagrams 79 – 84)

79: Yes
80: fXg6 e.p.
81: No; he is in check
82: He cannot castle queen side because of the black rook at d8 (you cannot castle *through* check); and he cannot castle on the king side because he would be moving into check from the bishop at c5.
83: Yes, with good play, two bishops can checkmate a lone king.
84: By perpetual check with Qc7+ Ka8 Qc8+ Ka7 Qc7+ etc.

9. Defend yourself! (MCSB) (Diagrams 109 – 112)

Diagram 109:
MOVE: Nc6, Ng6
CAPTURE: –
SUPPORT: d6, Bd6, Qf6, f6, Qe7
BLOCK: –
Bad moves: Nc4?, Nd3?, Nf3?, Ng4?, Qg5?

Diagram 110:
MOVE: b4
CAPTURE: –
SUPPORT: a6, Ba6, Bd7, Rb8, Qd7, Qb4
BLOCK: –
Bad moves: Qe8?, Qc5?, c6?, Nc3?

Diagram 111:
MOVE: Ra8, Rc8, Rb7, Rb4, RXb2
CAPTURE: NXg3
SUPPORT: all bad
BLOCK: f4, Nc7
Bad moves: Rb6?, Rb5?, Rb3?, Nf4?, Bd6?, Qd6?, Qc7?

Diagram 112:
MOVE: –
CAPTURE: –
SUPPORT: Qf6, Qe7, d6, Nc6, Bd6, f6
BLOCK: –
Bad moves: Qg5

A   Answers to the Final Test

1. QXb7
    QXc3
    BXg5
    BXh3
    bXc3
    NXc3
    NXc5
    NeXf6
    NeXg5
    KXe2
    NhXf6
    NhXg5

(Score 2 points for each correctly written capture)

2. (a) QXa5 (b) bXa4
        BXb6   BXf7+
        NXf5

(Score 2 points for each of these. Deduct 2 points for any other move).

3. Qg7++
    (5 points)

4. Rd8++
    (5 points)

5. (a) Rf8++ (b) Rb7
    (5 points each)

6. Rc6 (or Rc5, Rc4, Rc3, Rc2, Rc1)
    (5 points)

7. (a) Qf8++ (b) Qc7
    (5 points each)

8. (a) Qd7++   (b) Qe6
        Qf8++
    (5 points each)

9. (a) No
    (b) Yes
    (c) Yes
    (d) No
    (2 points each)

10. (a) c7 – c5
     (b) dXc6 e.p.
     (2 points each)

11. (a) The rook on f7 and the bishop on g4 are attacked.
     (b) NXg4
     (2 points for each part)

12. MOVE: Nc1, Nd4, Nf4
     CAPTURE: – (RXa6 is bad: deduct 2 points)
     SUPPORT: Rd2, Re1, Kf1, Bf1, Bf3
     BLOCK: c4 (Rd3 is bad: deduct 2 points)
(2 points for each move. Deduct 2 points each for any other moves)

13. (a) Qf6 (or Qe7)
     (b) To prevent QXf7++
(2 points each)

14. MOVE: Nd5, Nf5, Ng4 (all other knight moves are bad: deduct 2 points)
     CAPTURE: –
     SUPPORT: Re8, RXd3, Bc5
     BLOCK: –
(2 points for each move. Deduct 2 points each for any other moves).

15. (a) The rook on f7 and the bishop on c5 are attacked.
     (b) QXf7
(2 points for each part)

16. Any of the following moves is good:
     MOVE: Qa3, Qb5
     CAPTURE: QXh4
     SUPPORT: –
     BLOCK: Bb4, c4, Bc4, f4, g4
(2 points for each move. All other moves are bad: deduct 2 points for each of these)

17. Qe7!
     (5 points)

18. c8(R)!
     (5 points)

Maximum Score: 164 points

Pass Score: 123 points

Answers to supplementary exercises

1. Writing moves

1	2	3	4
Q✕a7	b✕c3	Rab1	Rae8
Rbe1	Q✕h6+	a4	b✕a4
Nb✕d4	Rd7	Rd8	Nce2
c✕d5	Rd1	Q✕b6	Q✕c7
Qf6	Nec4	Red1+	Qb1
h5	h4	N✕g6+	Nh5+

2. Seeing captures

1	2	3	4
B✕g8	K✕a3	N✕a3	a✕b6
Q✕a8+	b✕c6	R✕g8	B✕e7
Q✕a4	B✕a4	B✕a5	Q✕g5
Q✕e7	B✕e4	B✕h6	R✕e5
Q✕h7	R✕g1	N✕e7	N✕d3
R✕g3	N✕e7	Q✕b5	N✕g8
N✕h6	N✕h6	g✕h3	(6)
(7)	Q✕c7	(7)	
	Q✕g1		
	Q✕h4		
	(10)		

3. Value of the pieces

1)		2)	
N✕h6	(5)	B✕g7	(9)
R✕a1	(3)	b✕c7	(5)
B✕b8	(3)	Q✕e2	(5)
R✕e3	(1)	Q✕a6+	(3)
b✕c5	(1)	R✕h2	(3)
c✕b5	(1)	B✕a5	(1)
c✕d5	(1)	Q✕d5+	(1)
d✕c5	(1)	R✕h5	(1)
K✕g5	(1)	R✕a4	(1)
N✕e3	(1)		
(10)		(9)	

3)		4)	
R✕a7	(5)	N✕e2	(9)
R✕g4	(3)	B✕c8	(5)
R✕b8+	(3)	B✕e7	(5)
K✕c3	(3)	R✕h6	(3)
N✕c5	(1)	K✕h1	(3)
N✕e5	(1)	N✕b5	(1)
N✕g6	(1)	g✕h4	(1)
(7)		(7)	

4. Capture and recapture (1)

1			bad captures:	
R✕a8 B✕a8	(0)		N✕d7 Q✕d7	(−2)
N✕b6 Q✕b6	(0)			
B✕e7 N✕e7	(0)			
N✕c6 d✕c6	(0)			
N✕g6 h✕g6	(0)			
e✕f5 e✕f5	(0)			
h✕g7 K✕g7	(0)			

2			bad captures:	
Q✕a4 R✕a4	(0)		N✕e7 B✕e7	(−2)
c✕d6 c✕d6	(0)			
N✕c6 b✕c6	(0)			
N✕e6+ f✕e6	(0)			
N✕f6 e✕f6	(0)			
B✕h6+ K✕h6	(+2)			
h✕g4 h✕g4	(0)			

3			bad captures:	
a✕b4 a✕b4	(0)		Q✕c6 B✕c6	(−8)
B✕h8 R✕h8	(+2)			
B✕c8+ N✕c8	(+6)			
g✕h6 R✕h6	(+4)			

4			bad captures:	
N✕c7 N✕c7	(0)		N✕a7 K✕a7	(−2)
Q✕h5 B✕h5	(0)			
B✕g6 h✕g6	(0)			
d✕c5 b✕c5	(0)			
N✕d5 e✕d5	(0)			
B✕d8 R✕d8	(+2)			
a✕b6 a✕b6	(0)			

5. Capture and recapture (2)

1 bXa4 NXa4 (+2)   bad captures:
  BXa6 bXa6 (+2)   QXc7 QXc7 (−8)
  BXb6 RXb6 (0)
  NXd6 cXd6 (+6)
  RXf7 KXf7 (0)
  gXh4 NXh4 (0)

2 aXb6 cXb6 (0)   Bad captures:
  BXd3 NXd3 (0)   NXc7 RXc7 (−2)
  NXc5 bXc5 (0)   NXf6 gXf6 (−2)
  fXg4 hXg4 (+8)

3 NXd4 eXd4 (0)   bad captures:
  cXb6 cXb6 (0)   RXe5 dXe5 (−4)
  cXd6 cXd6 (0)   NXe5 dXe5 (−2)
  QXf8+ RXf8 (0)
  BXa8 QXa8 (+2)
  NXh6 KXh6 (+2)

4 dXc6 NXc6 (0)   bad captures:
  NXc8 QXc8 (0)   RXb4 RXb4 (−4)
  hXg6 hXg6 (0)   QXa6 BXa6 (−6)
  BXf8 KXf8 (+2)   NXf7 RXf7 (−2)

6. Getting out of check (1)

1 NXf2 2 Ne4 3 Kg5 4 KXd6 5 Bd3 6 QXf6

7. Getting out of check (2)

1 BXe7 2 BXg5 3 Bf3 4 KXe5 5 Nf5 6 BXe4

8. Checkmate (1)

1 Bc2++   2 Be8++   3 g6++
4 Ra7++   5 Nc5++   6 f5++

9. Checkmate (2)

1 Nf7++   2 Qe7++   3 Qf4++
4 Qg3++   5 Qb7++   6 Qd4++

10. Harder checkmates

1 Nf6++   2 Ne4++   3 Re6++
4 Be3++   5 Qe4++   6 Qd6++

11. MCSB (1)

1 MOVE: Ra2, Rc2, Rdd1 bad moves:
                 Rd3, Rd8+   Rb2? NXb2
                                Rd4? eXd4
                                Rd5? QXd5
                                Rd6? NXd6
                                Rd7? RXd7
      CAPTURE: BXc4
      SUPPORT: None   All supports are bad.
      BLOCK: None

2 MOVE: None
      CAPTURE: None
      SUPPORT: f6, d6, Nc6 bad support:
                 Bd6, Qe7, Qf6 Qg5? NXg5
      BLOCK: None.

3 MOVE: Na4, Nd1   bad moves:
                                  Nbc4? dXc4
                                  Nd3? eXd3
      CAPTURE: None
      SUPPORT: Rb1, Qb1, Qc1 bad supports:
                                  Ndc4? dXc4
      BLOCK: Nb3   bad block:
                                  Bb5? RXb5

4 MOVE: Qc2, Qd2,   bad moves:
                 Qb3, Qa4   Qe2? BXe2
                                  Qf3? BXf3
      CAPTURE: None   bad capture
                                QXg4? NXg4
      SUPPORT: None   All supports are bad.
      BLOCK: Nf3, Ne2, bad blocks:
                  Be2, f3   Re2? BXe2

12. MCSB (2)

1 MOVE: Bb3   bad moves:
                                   Ba6? R✕a6
                                   Bb5+? N✕b5
                                   Bd3? B✕d3

    CAPTURE: None   bad capture:
                                   B✕d5? Q✕d5

    SUPPORT: None
    BLOCK: None.

2 MOVE: Nf8, Nf6, Ne5 bad moves:
                                     Nb6? a✕b6
                                   Nc5? R✕c5

    CAPTURE: None   bad capture:
                                   Q✕h3? N✕h3

    SUPPORT: Kc8, Rd8, Qd6 bad support:
                                     Qc6? R✕c6

    BLOCK: e6   bad blocks:
                                   Qe6? B✕e6
                                   f5? B✕f5

3 MOVE: Na7, Nd6   bad moves:
                                     Na3? b✕a3
                                   Nc3? b✕c3
                                   Nd4? e✕d4

    CAPTURE: N✕f1
    SUPPORT: Rb8, Qb8, Qe8
                  Qd7, Qd5, Bd7, c6
    BLOCK: Bd3   bad blocks:
                                   Qd3? B✕d3
                                   Ne2? B✕e2

4 MOVE   Bd5, Bf5, Bg6 bad moves:
                 Bh7, B✕f3   Bb1? R✕b1
                                   Bc2? Q✕c2
                                   Bd3? Q✕d3

    CAPTURE: B✕c3
    SUPPORT: Re8, Qe8, Qe7 bad supports:
                 f5, Nf6   Qh4? N✕h4
                                   Nc5? d✕c5

    BLOCK: None